P9-ARZ-348

Any Given Day

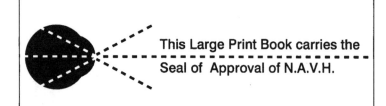

This Large Print Book carries the
Seal of Approval of N.A.V.H.

Any Given Day

THE LIFE AND TIMES OF
Jessie Lee Brown Foveaux

JESSIE LEE BROWN FOVEAUX

Thorndike Press • Thorndike, Maine

FALMOUTH PUBLIC LIBRARY
FALMOUTH, MA 02540-2895

Lg Print
920.042
Foveaux

Copyright © 1979, 1997 by Jessie Lee Brown Foveaux

All rights reserved.

Published in 1998 by arrangement with Warner Books, Inc.

Thorndike Large Print ® Basic Series.

The tree indicium is a trademark of Thorndike Press.

The text of this Large Print edition is unabridged.
Other aspects of the book may vary from the original edition.

Set in 16 pt. Plantin by Minnie B. Raven.

Printed in the United States on permanent paper.

Library of Congress Cataloging in Publication Data

Foveaux, Jessie Lee Brown, 1899–
    Any given day : the life and times of Jessie Lee Brown
Foveaux/ Jessie Lee Brown Foveaux.
        p. cm.
    ISBN 0-7862-1360-4 (lg. print : hc : alk. paper)
        1. Foveaux, Jessie Lee Brown, 1899–   . 2. Missouri
— Biography. I. Title.
    [CT275.F6868A3   1998]
    977.8'04'092—dc21
    [B]   97-47256

In publishing *Any Given Day*, we have tried to present to you the manuscript Jessie Lee Brown Foveaux originally wrote as faithfully as possible. Other than standard copyediting changes, Jessie Lee's words come to you here just as she wrote them for her family.

Hoping that some of my experiences may help them through trying times in their lives, and show them how easy it is to lose sight of the most worthwhile things in life. . . .

Introduction

Dear Grandchildren, Great-Grandchildren, and Grandchildren by marriage,

Some of you have asked me to tell you about my folks and how we used to live. Now that I am sure I won't have too many more years on this earth I had better get busy.

I'll try to give you a bird's-eye view of my life as I have lived it. I have joined a group of senior citizens or older people — whatever you wish to call us. We are interested in seeing what we can remember of the days gone by. If it sounds silly and rambling, so be it. I shall write these memories as they come to me. Many of these things have been forgotten for years; so here are the good and the bad days of my life. Some of you will perhaps laugh and toss this aside, some will read it through to the end.

Just remember — nothing is ever so bad it couldn't be worse. Most of my troubles have been my own fault. If one has faith, health, and the will to try, most problems can be solved. I almost let pride be the death of me. Too much is almost as bad as not enough. Anyway, I can't think of any-one I would change places with if I could.

In looking over my years, I think I have had a very rewarding life and hope you all may be as content and happy as I am in my twilight years. May your sunny days far outnumber the dark days of your lives. My wonderful family has been such a blessing to me. Each and every one of you is pre-cious to me; I love you very much. When I have left you, please remember how proud of all of you I am. Try to think of me in a great garden with beautiful flowers with no weeds to pull. Or maybe I can get a job as someone's guardian angel. If so, may I do as well as mine has done protecting me.

We have had some wonderful times to-gether. I treasure the memories so much. All the kind and thoughtful things you have all done. I feel that I am a very rich person indeed.

Never forget to take your troubles to a higher power than any on earth. It will pay off. I know.

Love,
Grandma Jessie Lee

Remember these lines:
For when the one Great Scorer comes to

write against your name, He will write not what you won or lost, but how you played the game.

Don't be influenced by what they call the Beautiful People. They are on a toboggan headed for a big crash.

Foreword

The great-great-grandparents of both my mother and father came to this wonderful country from Ireland. Some settled in Pennsylvania, others in Indiana, where all of them seemed to go after a few years. It was from Indiana that my mother's grandfather came to Kansas in covered wagons. They bought land near Laclede, Kansas, where they lived the rest of their lives. My dad's grandparents, father, and mother took another wagon train and went to Missouri, settling not too far from Kansas City, Missouri. They lived there until death and are buried near Latour, Missouri.

You will find all this and much more in the family tree. Hope you like it.

PART I

CHILDHOOD

(1899-1910)

Chapter 1

Margaret Pauley was the fourth child of Milton and Mary Ellen Pauley, and was born and raised in Manhattan, Kansas, Riley County. At the age of twenty years she had never been more than a few miles away from Manhattan.

The family consisted of two boys, Walter and Jesse, and seven girls — Margaret Olive

Margaret Olive (Pauley) Brown, Jessie Lee's mother, circa 1893 (approximately age 18).

(my mother), Rose, Louise, Daisy, Janette, Carrie, and Florence.

Mother had been taught to work at an early age, helping with the younger children as they came along and learning to cook and houseclean — all the things young girls should know.

Margaret was nineteen years old in 1896 and was in love (or thought she was) with a young man and they talked of marriage. There was only one thing keeping them apart. Harold and his family were Catholic. My mother's family were all Protestants. Both families were against the marriage.

So at last they parted to go their separate ways.

Chapter 2

Margaret had an uncle Jim Pauley, her father's brother, who had taken his family and moved to Missouri and were living in a little city called Quick City. It isn't a great deal larger now than it was then. Margaret wrote to them, asking if it would be convenient for her to come there for a short visit. Her aunt Oma soon answered, telling her to come on and stay as long as she liked.

So with her parents' blessing she said good-bye to friends and family and boarded the train for her journey. She was warmly welcomed by her relatives and she soon began to love the beautiful, quiet, little village and the kind friendly people she came to know. There were her cousins — Nettie, Riley, Frank, Lee, and Hattie, the youngest, who was a few years younger than Margaret. They all became great friends and Margaret stayed on.

She got some work around the countryside helping farm wives at harvesttime and when new babies arrived.

At church she met a young man named Almer Brown, a good-looking Irish lad with laughing brown eyes and a fun-loving disposition; he was always seeing the funny side of life. They became friends and started going out together, taking long buggy rides and going to parties held in the homes of friends.

(Sorry, my dears, no beer — guess you think they had dull lives. Well, they didn't think so.)

Chapter 3

On February 16, 1898, Almer Brown and Margaret Pauley were married in Holden, Missouri. They built a small house and settled down to a quiet, peaceful life.

In 1899 I came along to disrupt their peaceful existence, and Margaret came near to losing her life that stormy wild night. She awakened early on the morning of March 17 with pains. Daddy was worried because for two days it had been snowing and the roads were in very bad condition. Snow drifted so high no horse could pull a wagon or buggy over them, and Dr. Sheffer lived in Holden, ten miles away. Grandma came, and Aunt Cora Belle, Daddy's sister, and Mama's sister, Aunt Daisy, were there from Manhattan. Daddy hated to leave to go after the doctor, but they told him "to hurry and go on. We'll all stay and do what we can." Just as he was ready to start, Will Higgins, a neighbor boy about eighteen years old, came with his horse and said he would attempt to get the doctor. (In those days a doctor would go to a patient, or try to, at

*Jessie Lee Brown
at 3 months.*

any time.) So at ten o'clock that morning Will set out on that long ride.

The ladies did all they could for Mama, and they felt that as Grandma was a very good midwife who had assisted at many births, all alone when no doctor was there, all would be well.

Seems things have a way of going wrong when least expected. About ten P.M. that night Will and Dr. Sheffer came stumbling in, nearly frozen and very hungry. After getting warm by the big stove and eating, Dr. Sheffer went to work. I have been told my mother had a very difficult time, and when

I was born, they wrapped me up in a blanket and gave me to Aunt Cora Belle to care for. By the time they had Mama all taken care of it was well into the eighteenth of March.

It seemed that no one had remembered to look at the clock, so they didn't really know if I was born on the seventeenth or the eighteenth. Daddy, being Irish, insisted it was St. Patrick's Day. Aunt Daisy insisted it was the eighteenth. Maybe yes, maybe no. I will never know.

They decided to name me Jessie after a lovely lady named Jessie Fort and Mama's brother Jesse. Before they decided on a middle name, a young cousin of Mama's, Lee Pauley, came to see me. He was twelve years old and so disappointed that no one had named their baby for him. He had nieces and nephews and felt left out. Seemed all the young folks wanted a namesake at that time. He looked at me and said, "I know you won't name her Lee." Mama looked at his woebegone face and said, "Sure we will. That's just the name we need." So I became Jessie Lee Brown.

Chapter 4

They told me that my grandmother Mary Elizabeth (Molly) took charge of me and was very proud of me and my cousin Floyd. She kept us with her whenever she could. I have been told that she was a beautiful lady, a good friend, and always ready to help in times of trouble or illness.

She had four children: my father, Flemington Almer, called "F.A.," who had a twin brother who died in infancy; a daughter Cora Belle; and one named Dora Lee.

Aunt Cora Belle married Bert Higgins, a fine carpenter and a farmer.

Aunt Dora Lee married Mama's cousin Frank Pauley, so their children are both my first cousins and my third. I call them my double cousins.

When I was three months old we moved to Little Rock, Arkansas. Daddy was offered a job in a big sawmill there. He was to keep the machinery in good shape. So in June 1899, after placing our little house in the hands of my grandparents, we left for our new home. I never saw my grandmother again.

All I remember of the time we lived in Arkansas (it was called Arkan*saw* then) is what my parents told me. They said we lived in a house built on stilts or tall poles on the banks of the Old Black River (probably the Mississippi River). A long flight of wooden steps led to the small porch. The inside wasn't too bad after Mama arranged her things, which she'd had shipped on to us. They got their drinking water from the river. Everyone had an old iron kettle and on washdays a fire would be built under it. Then water was carried from the river and put into this kettle.

It was heated and added as needed to the washtub where the ladies scrubbed the clothes with a brush or their hands on an old washboard, the kind seen mostly now in museums. (I learned to wash clothes on an old washboard.)

After the white clothes had been scrubbed (lye soap was used), the clothes were placed in the black pot to boil and get the rest of the dirt out. Then into another tub of cold water.

After rinsing through this, they were put into a second tub of water for the final rinse. After that, some were starched, while some were put on clotheslines strung up between the trees and some were spread on the bushes to dry. Then the colored clothes were washed. It took all day and was a very tiring job. No wonder the women died young.

(Aren't you girls glad you live now and have your nice washers and dryers?)

My mother, who had never lived like this, found it hard to adjust. The people were different from the ones she had known in Kansas or Missouri.

Mama had baked cakes, cookies, and lightbread, as they called it, in a little oven in her wood stove. She used a starter for the bread, which she kept in a fruit jar or stone jar. These people didn't understand her ways, and she sure didn't understand theirs. They seemed to live on cornpone, baked sweet potatoes or yams, and cabbage and fatback, as they called it. Mama learned a lot from them, as they did from her. She taught them to bake bread, cakes, and cookies. They taught her to cook out of doors, bake the potatoes in hot ashes, cook food in the fireplace, and make cornpone and sour milk biscuits. They took her into the countryside to pick huckleberries, blackberries, and wild strawberries. (I would have liked that.)

Chapter 5

Our nearest neighbors were a family named Mosely. They had one daughter named Pearl. My parents liked them very much. Mr. Mosely worked at the mill with my father. Pearl spent a lot of time at our home talking with Mama and playing with me. She taught me to walk before I was eight months old. Daddy and Mr. Mosely liked to fish and set lines along the riverbank at night, hoping to catch some of the large ones. Daddy heard them tell how some had been caught weighing fifty and sixty-five pounds. He was determined to get one of those.

Mama told me that one morning Dad had to go to work real early to fix some machinery and didn't have time to go check his lines. Mr. Mosely said he would go and see if they caught anything, and sure enough, this was the day.

Mr. Mosely called to someone to come help him get the fish on the bank. At last he and some neighbors had it safe on shore and were admiring it, when a young doctor who cared for the people at the mill came and decided he would clean the fish right then and there.

Mama had joined the crowd by this time, and she and Mr. Mosely begged him to leave it alone until Daddy could get there to see it.

But the doctor said, "No, he won't care. He'll be glad it is all cleaned up," and proceeded to go to work on it. Then he passed portions to those standing around.

Mama took hers and went home to wait for the explosion that she knew would come when her man came home.

Sure enough, his Irish temper took over, and Mama said she thought that doctor had seen his last day. Daddy had tried so hard to get a big fish and then not to be able to see anything except the head and tail was too much.

Daddy had a friend who had a riverboat and made trips up and down the Mississippi River to New Orleans. When Daddy could get away he would take us along. The family really enjoyed these trips.

My mother and the other ladies planned a picnic one time. She said she made potato salad and baked beans, getting all the things ready for a picnic like at home.

When it was time to eat she was so surprised to see pots of cold cabbage, sweet potatoes, cornpone, and cold biscuits.

They roasted corn somehow, but I never learned how. I can just see the flies and mosquitoes buzzing around.

Chapter 6

One day Daddy, who always saw the funny side of things, met a man who was in Little Rock trying to buy pearls. It seemed that the large river mussels or clamshells sometimes had nice pearls in them.

These men would come here and buy them from the people for very little money, then take them to the cities and make a nice profit on them.

He asked Daddy if he knew of anyone who had some nice pearls. Daddy pretended to think hard for a while, then said, "Well, I do know one man who has a pearl, but I don't think he will sell it."

The man then said, "Please give me his name and address and I'll go see him this evening. If it is a good one, I'll pay well."

Then the man wrote the address on a paper, thanked Daddy, and left.

Daddy hurried to find Mr. Mosely and tell him of the joke they could play on the pearl buyer. He was all for it.

That evening he answered the knock on his door and the salesman said, "I met a man today who told me you had a nice pearl. Will you sell it?"

"No, I reckon not," said Mr. Mosely.

"Well, then, can I see it?"

"Oh, I reckon that's all right," and he called out, "Pearl! Come in here," and in came daughter Pearl, a very pretty sixteen-year-old girl.

The salesman turned and fled into the night. They never saw him again.

Chapter 7

There were lots of trees growing around the house. Many kinds of birds lived in them, also hoot owls. They say one of the first things I learned to do was to hoot like an owl and awaken my parents much too early in the mornings.

Late in 1900 when I was a little over one year old my mother and I both got the malaria fever, and I had it each year thereafter until I was sixteen years old.

In the fall of 1900, we moved to Manhattan, Kansas. My first trip to Manhattan we stayed a few weeks with Mama's parents. (Of course I don't remember any of this. All I know of those days Mama told me much later.) Daddy couldn't find work, so he went to a farm near Omaha, Nebraska. It was very cold there.

Mama said they had very little fuel, only corncobs and some wood. She told me how hard it was keeping fires going in a cookstove and heating with coals, and whenever I pass through Nebraska I try to picture an old house standing all alone with a few trees as wind shelter and my parents trying to keep from starving and freezing that winter so long ago.

Chapter 8

In August of 1901 we returned to Manhattan. Mama was expecting another child. We were staying with her parents until after the birth. Daddy found some work, but nothing he liked.

Several of my father's relatives had gone

to Anacortes, Washington, where there was plenty of work, the kind my father liked, in sawmills. Anacortes was a little town on the Fidelgo Bay across from Seattle. Daddy's sister Cora Belle and her husband, as well as a cousin, Robert Moore, and some aunts and uncles were all there and liked it very much. They wrote, begging Daddy to come as soon as he could.

My only sister was born on October 1, 1901. I was two and a half years old. When she was a few days old Daddy shipped our things and took off. We would follow as soon as Mama was able to travel. Dr. Silkman was the family doctor, and when he said Mama was strong enough we started, my sister Teresa Elizabeth, Mama, and I. It was a long, long journey.

The only thing I remember of that trip is that when we arrived in Seattle my father was there to meet us. And how glad I was to see him again! Mama told me how good the other passengers were to help her take care of Tressie and me. It took several days to make the trip. She didn't know how she would have managed without their help.

Daddy got our luggage and a man with a red cap on his head helped us into a spring wagon with a horse hitched to it. That took us to the boat.

Jessie Lee Brown, 2 years old.

It didn't take long to cross the bay to Anacortes, and at the dock our relatives were waiting to welcome us.

We stayed with Aunt Cora Belle and Uncle Bert for a few days, then moved into the new home for us that Daddy had rented at the edge of town.

It was a fruit farm owned by a Mr. Amos, who sold most of the fruit. He told us to use all we wanted, and we did. Wonder it didn't make me sick, I ate so much of it while we lived there.

Chapter 9

We loved that old house and settled into a happy life there. The house had a large, friendly kitchen with several windows, built-in cupboards, and a large pantry. From the windows one could see the lovely fruit trees. When they were in bloom, it was one of the most beautiful sights you can imagine.

The wonderful living room I shall never forget. It had large windows across the end facing the bay. Under the windows was a long window seat, padded and covered with soft green cloth that could be taken off and washed. It looked more like a divan. Mama had piled pretty cushions on it. It was so nice to sit there and watch the boats go sailing by. When it was windy the waves splashed so high; the water looked all green and blue and white. From our window the beach looked to be very close by. In fact, it was over a block away.

It was such a nice, cheery place, that home of ours, and how we loved it.

The yard was filled with beautiful roses. Dark red ones that were called Jack roses and looked like velvet. Then the most gorgeous yellow ones, long slender buds that burst into large yellow blossoms too beautiful to pick. Then the white roses and the pink ones — to me a paradise. Next came the pansies with their purples and golds and as large across as a teacup.

Best of all to me was the fruit, greengage plums (large purple ones), the kind prunes are made of. Pears, apples, several kinds. Cherries — the large Bing cherry and a white one with pink color on it. Makes me hungry to think of them.

Next came a very large blackberry bush, large as a room, taking up one corner of the backyard. It was called the ever-bearing blackberry and had berries all except three months a year.

Chapter 10

I was so fond of apples that I didn't always wait until they were ripe. Mama told me not to eat any until she said I could.

One day the temptation was too great. They looked so pretty I thought they had to be good, so I walked to that tree and pulled one off and started to eat it.

One of Daddy's young cousins was in the house talking to Mama, Fred Moore was his name. He was fifteen or sixteen years old and tall; looked like a man to me.

Mama had told him that she didn't know how to keep me out of the apples until they were ready to eat, she was afraid I would get sick.

So Freddy had a wonderful cure for me. He would scare me into leaving them alone.

He went to a closet at the back of the house where old coats were kept. He got a long black coat and an old hat and took a long scarf and wrapped it around his face enough that I wouldn't know him. He pulled the hat low on his forehead and quietly went out the back door.

He came around the side of the house where I was enjoying the apple and said, "Jessie Lee, I am the devil! I get little girls and boys who don't mind their mothers. I take them away and they never get back. Didn't your mama tell you not to eat those apples?"

I stammered out, "Yes sir."

He said, "Well, I guess I will have to take you with me."

I started screaming and kept it up until I was hysterical. My mama came running out and Fred left very fast.

I told Mama as soon as I could talk that the devil was going to take me far away. She said she would talk to him and tell him I'd mind what I was told after this. And I did.

For a long time I had nightmares and wouldn't go near those trees.

Mama later let Freddy know that she disapproved of his cure method very much.

My daddy was so angry with Freddy that he threatened dire things if he ever frightened any of his children again.

Years later Fred and I laughed about it and he said, "You were scared — what about me? I thought F.A. would kill me!" Anyway, I have never stolen an apple since that day.

Chapter 11

When Tressie and I were old enough to be out in the yard, Daddy brought home a big beautiful shepherd dog. He was well trained as a watchdog and gentle with children.

Mama would say, "Now, Shep, you watch the girls and don't let them outside the yard." He seemed to understand; if we went too far away, he would grab hold of our dress and pull us back.

We loved him so much.

We had several cousins who came often to play with us while our mothers sewed, quilted, or just visited. The mothers made all our clothing.

My sister and I soon began to disagree, as most sisters do. We were so different. She was a little butterball, nearly as broad as she was long, with beautiful dark brown eyes and a fiery temper. I was so skinny that I had to stand twice in the same spot to make a shadow. I had blond hair and blue eyes. I liked dolls and pretty trinkets. She liked anything I didn't.

Mama tried to make our dresses to hide our defects. Mine had ruffles and lace to try to camouflage my thinness. Tressie's were made to make her seem not so plump. Well, now, Tressie wanted ruffles. (Poor Mama.) Men seemed to prefer her to me in those days, because of her temper, I guess. She would flare up in an instant, those brown eyes shooting sparks. They enjoyed getting her started.

I didn't get angry often, didn't need to. By the time I was five years old I had learned that a smile goes a long, long way.

By being friendly and happy-go-lucky, I nearly always got my way without a fit of anger.

I learned at an early age that if I wanted to do something and asked when Mama was tired, she said no. But if I waited another day, and asked when she wasn't busy, I nearly always got to do what I wanted — so why waste energy by throwing a fit?

I had heard Mama say that honey catches more flies than vinegar. I used to wonder what that meant. Now I know.

I have always liked people from the time I can remember and have had so many wonderful friends.

Chapter 12

Those were happy times.

In the little town of Anacortes, as I remember, it was quite primitive. We couldn't leave our yard because brush grew all around and a child could get lost very easily. Also little branches of water had to be crossed to get to town or most neighbors' homes.

Our yard was fenced all the way around.

We never went outside that fence alone.

On Sundays and holidays we would go to the beach and attend clambakes along the shore. The Indians knew how to fix them, and crowds would gather to eat them. Evenings we often went to the beach below our home, and Tressie and I would play in the sand and pick up pretty shells and pebbles. We always took along little pails to put them in. Daddy would dig clams with a shovel. Sometimes he would put us in an old rowboat and pull us along in the water; we would get all wet and dirty, and go home taking our little buckets of shells and the clams. Mama was waiting to give us a bath and put us to bed.

One day we were taken to the home of our cousins Lillie and Bob Moore. We were told we could stay overnight, our first night away from Mama.

Lillie let us play until we were tired out and too sleepy to care where we were. Then she put us to bed.

Her son, Clyde, was my age and we were the best of friends.

I remember the next morning we walked through the brush to our house. It was the Fourth of July 1903. Such a beautiful morning — the birds flying out of the bushes as we came along and us trying to catch them.

At home we opened the door and there stood Aunt Cora Belle with a bundle in her arms wrapped in my own special little blanket. Daddy's cousin Stella was there too. Not Mama.

I just stood there and stared at them, and Aunt Cora Belle said, "Come here, girls and see your new little brother."

Tressie said, "We don't want a brother," and I said, "What is he doing in my blanket?"

Stella said, "I didn't know it was your blanket. I'll get another."

We didn't think much of that baby. I remember asking where Mama was and I was told that she was sleeping.

Then I asked where they got that baby and I was told that Dr. Applebee brought him over from Bellingham on the boat. (They didn't want to discuss the birds and the bees with me.) I asked why he didn't give him to Aunt Cora Belle and Uncle Bert; they said they wanted a baby.

Stella said, "Oh, well, your daddy wanted a boy to grow up and help him in the mill."

They named him Harvard Lynn.

Mama, who was never very strong, was a long time getting well. Cousin Stella, who was a nurse, stayed as long as she could. Then our great-grandmother Molly Brown came from Missouri to stay with us.

She was a tiny little dark-eyed lady with lovely white hair. She wore it in curls high on her head with pretty combs to hold it. We all loved her so much. She had a great sense of humor and a way of getting things done, and was so good to us.

Lillie and Aunt Cora Belle did the laundry and helped where they could. One thing sure — we had plenty of help, all those relatives of my dad. Uncle John Chitwood and Aunt Ann. Uncle Bascom Moore and Aunt Adaline. All their families. Who needed hospitals? We had family and good doctors who would come day or night, rain or shine.

Chapter 13

Mama got strong enough to take over, Great-Grandma went back to Missouri, and we settled back to a happy, contented existence.

That fall we got the whooping cough; all the children did who hadn't already had it.

Tressie got it first. She seemed not to feel so well one morning, coughed some but not hard. Mama said she was coming down

Jessie Lee's great-grandparents Mary Elizabeth (Mollie) and Isaac Brown.

with a cold, so she made her stay inside. That night she whooped hard and they decided she had the whooping cough. Next day, one more whoop and no more. She was over it.

Then I got it. High fever, runny nose, watery eyes, and coughing, all getting worse as the day went by.

Next morning Dr. Applebee came and said, "Yes, Margaret, she has the whooping cough. Keep her in bed till we get this fever down."

The cough got worse. I took calomel, the fever medicine. The fever left, but not the cough. I coughed until I was so weak and skinny I had to stay in bed. At last it left as silently as it had come.

The next year Stella was taking a vacation from the hospital in Bellingham. That place was raging with scarlet fever. Stella had nursed some children who had it, so soon after she came we got that. She thought she had brought it to us, the germs in her clothing — anyway, it was after she came and held us in her lap that we got it.

Again Tressie had a very light case of it, some fever, a rash that soon disappeared.

Then came my turn. I nearly died. Poor Stella felt so bad, she stayed to take care of me. Said it was all her fault. Of course, it wasn't.

Dr. Applebee said I couldn't live, the fever would kill me. My daddy said I would make it, so here I am.

Daddy took a large pillow and laid me on it and carried me out in the sunshine. He would feed me a spoonful of whatever Dr. Applebee said I should have until I gained some strength.

I got well fast once I started to recover, but Mama said no matter what they gave me I stayed skinny.

Chapter 14

We loved going shopping in the little town with its shops all in rows and the wooden sidewalks. The stores seemed like fairyland to us. So many things were made by the Indians. The Indians traded buckskin slippers, long chains of bright colored beads, and shells of all kinds, and on those trips we would get some candy.

There was a Chinaman who had a laundry. They called him Old John, I suppose because they couldn't say his right name. He wore his hair in a queue down his back, wore wide-leg trousers, and the sleeves of his shirts or blouses were long and wide. He had a nice, friendly smile.

One night some good-for-nothing men killed poor John and threw him down a deep well, not far from where we lived. It worried me quite a bit. I would wonder if all the blood came out of him into that water. They said whoever did this crime cut him up. Then I couldn't figure out how anyone knew he was in the well — all sorts of things. Children were not to ask questions about things like that.

Seemed all kinds of exciting things were happening. One night the Thompson Saw Mill (the one we could see so plainly from our living room) started burning.

Great billows of flame and smoke were shooting up into the skies, large planks falling into the water with great splashes. Whistles blowing, tugboats crying out warnings into the dark night — it was a fascinating sight to behold.

I spent almost all my time at that window watching. Never since have I witnessed a fire like that, and I pray I never will. The dry kilns burned for months.

The flames had flashed into the sky so high — near heaven, I thought, and I hoped none of the angels would be burned. To me, angels were little people who lived in heaven and flew around at night looking into windows to see if the children were sleeping and safe from harm.

I also spent a lot of energy trying to catch birds. My uncle Bert told me that if I would take a salt shaker out and slip up to the bushes and sprinkle salt on their tails, I could catch me some.

Of course I tried, but they always got away.

But Uncle Bert had fun —

I wish you could have known him. He was a real comic. He made one happy just to have him around, and he loved kids. He was never too busy or too tired to tell us stories or take us for long walks.

Sometimes we would get to playing a little too rough to suit Cora Belle and she would say, "Now, Bert, you be careful. Those children will get hurt."

He would say, "No, they won't. They are not made of china-ware — they won't break into pieces."

Aunt Adaline was the news carrier. She would go from one family to another, gathering all the gossip and telling what she heard before. We didn't need a newspaper.

Mama and Aunt Cora used to hide if they saw her coming, when they had anything they wanted to get done. They said once Addie got started, there was no stopping her.

Her kids were all grown up. Guess she didn't have enough to keep her busy.

Chapter 15

There was an old man who peddled fish who came by our house two or three times a week. He had a big old cart he pushed along. I'd run out to stop him until Mama could get some money and come to buy some fresh fish.

He would yell, "Fish, fresh fish. Salmon, halibut, smelt, clams!" and sometimes he had large crabs. We liked those best. They had large claws or legs, and that's the part eaten. They were put into a pot of boiling water and boiled. I don't know how Mama knew when they were done. The shells were cracked and broken and the meat was so good. Wish I had some now.

Everyone liked living in Washington. It was truly the land of the free.

Daddy had a job he liked very much at a mill only a short distance from home. He had bought some timberland that he planned to clear and build a home on someday.

I doubt if we would have ever left there if Mama had been well. She never did get really strong after Lynn's birth, and now she was getting worse; she couldn't breathe right.

Lynn had a deformed foot or enlarged anklebone. Anyway, he couldn't walk with it, so they put braces on it. It was when they took him to Bellingham to get the brace that Mama went to a specialist.

After examining her, he declared that she would have to leave the climate. It was very damp there, raining some most every day. He said if she stayed in Washington, she wouldn't live long.

Dr. Applebee had already told her this. She came home and told Daddy what this new doctor had said.

Daddy loved his work and the state, but Mama came first. So he put his land up for sale and in 1905 made plans to move back to Missouri. Time passed.

Chapter 16

We received word that Grandma Brown, Daddy's mother, had died in her sleep. Grandpa wanted us to come home to Missouri.

I could not quite understand at age six just what dying meant. We had a little old lady who lived in a big old house across the street. We called it "the Mystery House." No one seemed to know much about Mrs. White; she stayed by herself and didn't seem to want friends.

The house was painted white with large green shutters on the windows, which she always kept closed on our side. She had a white picket fence all around it. We never saw anyone go there.

If Tressie and I were playing close enough to hear her, she would call us to the fence and give us cookies and large bouquets of her lovely pansies. We liked her very much.

Then we didn't see her outside for several days. We were told she had died.

We saw carriages arrive and people get out and go in. Mama said it was people who had come for her funeral.

I wondered what a funeral was. Tressie and I were in the front yard, watching to see what would happen.

A long black wagon or carriage with two beautiful dark gray horses pulling it stopped at the house. More people came in horse-pulled buggies and went into the house.

After a long while, we saw some men carrying a long box out of the house and put it in the carriage with the gray horses. Then the rest of the people came out, got in their carriages, and all came right by our house and on past.

We watched until we couldn't see them anymore. I wondered where they were taking her and went in to ask Mama.

She told me that those people had been friends or relatives of Mrs. White's, and that they had gone into the house and had the funeral.

I wanted to know what that was and how they did it.

She said, "Sit down and be quiet a minute, Jumping Jack, and I'll try to explain it."

She told me they had come to say good-bye to her for the last time, to say prayers, and that a preacher had perhaps said a few things about her long life, and now they were taking her to the cemetery.

She said that the black carriage was called a hearse and was used only for funerals, that Mrs. White's body was in the long box and had been taken to the cemetery.

I wanted to know what that was, and she said a resting place for those who die, where the Lord will come for them someday.

I asked if they took my grandma in one of those wagons, too, and she said, "Yes, honey, your grandma Brown is resting in Rose Hill Cemetery in Missouri." (And a beautiful place it is, too.)

I asked if I could go and see the place when we went to Missouri, and she said, "Sure you can."

I thought it was all right if the Lord knew where they were and was coming back to get them.

It never was quite the same with Mrs. White gone. No more cookies and pansies, and I had liked talking to her. Wish I could remember what she had said. Only thing I can recall is, "Be a good girl now."

Chapter 17

Mama was teaching me to read. I knew my ABC's, and could count, and could read some of the lines in my little books.

There were no schools close enough for me to go to, and we were preparing to leave anyway. Mama was a good teacher.

Cousin Clyde was my best friend; we played together hours at a time. We had some make-believe friends we called Deet and Dom.

Anything that went wrong for us we blamed on Deet and Dom. We would insist it was their fault if we didn't mind our parents. Mama wanted to know where and who they were.

How could we tell her when we didn't know ourselves? They were just imaginary friends.

I had a habit of biting my fingernails. Mama tried everything she heard of . . . nothing worked. Then Jenny Hogan, a cousin of Daddy's, came to visit her parents, Aunt Ann and Uncle Bob Chitwood.

She brought boxes of shells and beads. She cleaned the shells with an acid, washed them off good, and they were so pretty. It was a long process, but she sold many of them. I was fascinated by them.

Jenny said, "Jessie Lee, if you will stop biting those fingernails, you may have some shells for your very own."

Greed took over. I wanted those shells and beads so much that every time my hand went to my mouth I'd seem to hear Jenny say, "You will never get my shells."

Well, she was wrong. As soon as I could prove to her that I had fingernails again, she paid up. (I still have some of those shells.) A bad habit was gone forever.

Chapter 18

At last things were in order and time was drawing near to leave. Oh, how we hated to leave, to even think of going away from our pretty home, friends, and relatives.

Daddy wanted to get started, so we had a sale, and sold a lot of our things, and shipped the rest to Missouri.

I was a selfish little lady, and didn't want to part with my things. I had a red wagon that was my pride and joy.

Mama said it would have to be sold. I had so many dolls, she wanted to give them away.

I made such a fuss that Daddy said my dolls could go.

The morning of the sale, my little red wagon was bought for a little boy I had never seen before.

He started to climb into it with a glass of milk in his hand and spilled it all over my wagon.

I ran to the house, yelling, "I hate that boy! He ruined my wagon!"

I was promised another when we got to Missouri.

Then there was the grief of giving up old Shep. He looked so sad, like he knew we were leaving him. That was the worst part of going.

Before we left the house an Indian friend, Charlie Beal, who lived close by, came to the door with beautiful hand-beaded moccasins for Tressie and me. They were made of deerskin. The flood of 1951 took mine. . . .

We hated to say good-bye to Charlie. He had been a good friend, often bringing us venison roasts and steaks.

Never again could we watch the canoe races; those Indian boys worked so hard to win.

Never again could we hear the mournful whistle of the tugboats as they made their way through the dense fog at night.

Chapter 19

The day came to lock the door of our little home for the last time.

We went to Aunt Cora Belle's home to stay until the boat would dock to take us to Seattle to get on the train. It was a day or two, I guess.

Then came the last good-byes. (I always hated that — still do.)

We were being taken from a place we loved, to what?

After promising to return to visit, we were at last on our way. The ship was like a big house floating on the water. It kept moving faster, and soon Anacortes was far behind us forever. None of us has ever returned. No use now . . . too many changes. To me, it is like I left it, fall of 1906.

Tressie and I liked the boat ride; Lynn didn't seem to care. He was a quiet kid who played by himself most of the time.

At the depot in Seattle where Daddy bought the tickets, he told the man that I was seven years old. Any child over six years was supposed to pay half fare.

The man said, "She looks more like four to me, so go on," so I came home free.

The train was quite an experience for Tressie, Lynn, and me, whizzing along the tracks so fast, looking out the windows, and eating our meals on the train. We had brought a huge basket of food and enough fruit to last a month.

They made beds for us at night. The conductor and porter were real friendly, also the passengers.

All went well until we were high up in

the mountains, then Mama started having what seemed to be heart attacks.

There happened to be a doctor on board, and he took over.

The passengers took care of Tressie, Lynn, and me.

I remember some of the people fanning her with a newspaper so she could breathe. Daddy was so frightened. The doctor said once we were on level ground again he thought Mama would feel much better.

By the time we reached Kansas City, she was able to walk into the depot.

We had another long wait for a train.

It would be a long, long time before I saw mountains again, or saw waves on the ocean, and never again have I seen flowers and fruit like the ones we left in Washington.

Chapter 20

Now Missouri was a different story.

We found a lot of relatives here of both my parents. We were so tired when we got to Quick City and my grandfather's home, it took a few days to get settled down again.

It was fun getting to know the relatives; there were new cousins to play with.

It sure wasn't our beloved Washington. The weather here was hot and it rained a lot, sometimes days at a time. In Anacortes it rained a shower, then cleared and was nice. Here it poured down.

It had never lightninged or thundered in Anacortes, so the first time I saw the lightning I was scared out of my senses. I crawled under a bed and hid my face. (Thinking like the ostrich, I guess, that if I couldn't see it, I was safe. So I buried my head in the sand.) I still don't like thunderstorms.

It seems that we were always going to the storm cellar. Everyone had a large cave dug into the ground, with a lot of dirt on top of it. It had a strong wooden frame under the dirt to keep it from falling in. Then it had a large wooden door and steps were built going down into this dark, gloomy room where the canned fruit, jams, and jellies were kept, also great stone jars of pickles and sauerkraut.

There was always a cot, a chair or two, and a small table, and on the door frame hung two large lanterns, kept filled with kerosene, with matches in a tin box fastened to the wood above the door.

The grown-ups had to bend down to keep from hitting their heads as they entered this place. It was cold and smelled musty, but we couldn't see that awful lightning, which never seemed to bother my sister.

After a short stay with Grandpa, Daddy got a job with an old friend and schoolmate, Cyrus Farnsorth. He had two wonderful farms and needed a man to help him, so we moved to "the house on the hill." This was where the large fruit orchards were.

Daddy didn't get much money, but was furnished with the house and a cow. It was a fine place for pigs and chickens and had a nice garden space.

With all that fruit who needed much money? The garden had Concord grapes across one side. The garden was fenced in to keep the chickens out.

Chapter 21

Cyrus and his wife, Cynthia, had two children: Bonnie, my age, and a little boy, Jewel, who was Lynn's age. (He grew up to be a very good doctor and practiced medicine and surgery in Kansas City, Missouri.

He was still there, last I heard.) Our families spent a lot of time together.

We were always glad to go to their home. They had large barns, windmills, dogs, cats, and little lambs. Cyrus kept a lot of sheep. We could watch the sheep being sheared of their wool in the spring and the barn swallows flying about.

Every day was a happy day. Bonnie and Jewel were like cousins; we called their parents Uncle Cy and Aunt Cynthy.

After harvest Mama and Aunt Cynthy would have the men take the mattresses off all the beds and carry them to a place not in use, then empty them of the straw they had been filled with. Then they washed the covers, and when dry, they got busy and filled them with nice clean straw and carried them back to the house, where they sewed across the open end and put them back on the beds until next harvesttime. They were so nice to sleep on.

When it was canning time, Mama, Aunt Cynthy, and some friends would come to our home, as that's where the fruit was. The ladies brought their jars. They put big wash boilers of water on the kitchen range and boiled jars, while they prepared the fruit for canning.

There were no kitchen sinks or running

water in those days. Everyone had a deep well all boxed in with a lid on it. It was built up about four or five feet from the ground, to protect children and animals and keep dirt and trash from blowing in. Each well had one or two old oaken buckets on chains or heavy ropes over a pulley that was fastened to a log over the top of the frame. There were always tin cups or gourd dippers hanging on the well frame. The bucket was lowered into the water and pulled back up.

It was a very tiresome job on washdays or when a lot of water was needed.

Some days the ladies would make peach, plum, or apple butter.

A fire was started under a huge black kettle, which was propped up on large rocks. The fruit was put into the kettle, a fire started, and soon the sweet smell of sugar and spice plus the fruit filled the air.

It had to be stirred constantly, and that's when the oldest children were put to work, stirring with a large wooden paddle. Of course, one of the mothers inspected often to make sure it didn't scorch.

It wasn't much fun. We were tired almost as soon as we started, and it changed hands often. When the ladies finished the work inside, they took over and we were free to go play.

We loved those days our mothers worked together; all the children were brought along. We had such good times.

It would be late in the evening when the jars were filled and divided. The ladies were tired but happy to have done a good day's work.

This was repeated until they had all the fruit needed for the winter. Then Uncle Cy left word at the store in the village that anyone wanting the rest of the fruit could come and pick it. If any was left, we turned the pigs into the orchard.

I remember the days we had large racks of apples, peaches, or corn drying in the sun.

The men took several long boards and put them on what they called sawhorses. They were covered with yards of un-bleached muslin. The fruit was spread over them and covered with cheesecloth or mosquito netting.

Mama and Daddy carried them into the smokehouse at night and put them back in the sun the next day. I don't remember it raining on them.

Blackberry picking was another fun time. Large tubs, buckets, anything to hold berries, were loaded into the big farm wagons. Children were put in with blankets and baskets of food and jugs of water, and off we would go with two or three other families, to spend the day picking berries.

The men wore high-topped boots and took long sticks to beat around the area to make sure there were no rattlesnakes hiding in the bushes.

The children were told to stay by the wagons under the trees and play. The oldest children were to watch out for the younger ones. We didn't like that much. Later came the nice picnic lunch and visiting while the grown-ups rested awhile.

About sundown, with all the containers filled, a wagonload of tired, sleepy children went home.

Those berries were so large and juicy and free for the picking. Next day jelly was made or the berries were canned for pies.

Chapter 22

Fall came. Time for school to start. It was 1907, I would be eight in the spring, and I had never been inside a schoolhouse. I was anxious to go.

The school was a mile and a half from

our home. Of course, Bonnie would go there too.

The teacher was Miss Jessie McKay. She stayed at the home of Uncle Cy and Aunt Cynthy, so she would walk with us.

Miss McKay and Bonnie walked across the sheep pasture to our place, then we took a shortcut through the orchards to the road.

The school was on a hill and was called Possum Trot. Going up that hill was work. Coming down was fun.

Just before getting to the school we had another old orchard to go through; it was another shortcut.

It was owned by Morris Quick. They had abandoned this old farm and it was fast deteriorating. He had a daughter Clara, in the school, and another, Edith, going to college in Warrensburg, besides sons Neil, Lawrence, and Paul.

The orchard still had fruit in it, and other things not so nice, such as nettles, bees, and little animals scurrying around.

Next came the creek we must cross. We liked that and played there at noontime and recess. Wild onions and pretty flowers grew along the banks. You all know how I like onions! Well, I ate those too. (Poor teacher.)

Then on up the hill to the old white schoolhouse.

The school had a long porch across the front with the door in the middle of the building. Inside, it was one large room.

At the back end was a closet with some shelves for our lunch buckets and hooks for our coats. Below the shelves we put our overshoes.

There was a large round stove in the center of the room. Long windows were on each side of the room, with the blackboard on the front wall, and the teacher's desk and chair, some pictures on the walls, and in the corner some shelves for books. Hanging on the walls in wall brackets were some kerosene lamps, for use when meetings were held there at night. Besides our desks, that was *it*.

Miss McKay had grades from one to eight, and some of the students were sixteen to eighteen years old. They often had to miss school and help on their parents' farms. Then they had to catch up as they could.

I started in first grade, but was put into second in a few days as Mama had taught me the first grade work at home. I was the smallest one there, and the older children always looked after me.

School was fun. First thing after roll call Miss McKay read us a Bible story. Then we sang some songs, one being "Way Down upon the Swanee River." I liked that one best, even though I used to get the words mixed up a bit. I was saying "Where my heart is turning yellow" instead of "ever," until someone told me.

I had trouble hearing sometimes; my ears had what they called "gathering," and until they healed I didn't always get things straight in my head.

Our outhouse was down the hill by the creek. The boys had one on the other side of the schoolhouse.

It was one small room with a long bench on one side with round holes cut in it, made like all the outhouses, as we called them. No one had a bathroom then.

The one at school had wasps, or "was-rups," as I called them, and I hated to go there. I was so afraid of wasps.

I still wonder how we managed to walk at all with all the clothing we wore in the winter. First the long underwear, with heavy wool stockings fastened to it with garters. Next came outing flannel bloomers or black sateen, then two petticoats, and a long wool dress. Last came stocking caps, a big heavy coat, and a muffler. Our mittens were on a long string that we slipped around our neck, then into the sleeves of our coats. This way we couldn't lose them. If we fell down, we had to help one another up again.

How did we ever play fox and geese in the snow? In case none of you know, it is played by choosing a fox, who hid behind a tree or someplace. The rest are the geese. The fox tries to catch the geese and put them into his pen. They must stay there until he catches all of them or the bell rings. We built snowmen and snowhouses, played drop the handkerchief, and "London Bridge Is Falling Down." How we ever did it in all those clothes is a mystery to me.

Chapter 23

We were liking Missouri and the people more and more.

Mama was very busy. A farm wife has very little time for anything except work.

Sundays were special. The trip to church, visiting with friends and neighbors, catching up on the news, seemed to revive my mother and the other farm wives, giving them strength for a new week.

The next year, Tressie wanted to go to school too, so she started.

Mama hadn't had much luck trying to teach her. She wanted to play.

Miss McKay made the mistake of letting Tressie take an old doll to school with her. She played with it and didn't pay attention.

One day Miss McKay took the doll and told Tressie that if she didn't pay attention and put that doll away until playtime, she would take it away and burn it.

Tressie was a sassy little creature; she said, "When she gets as old and cranky as you are, I'll burn her myself."

Miss McKay took the doll and put it on the highest shelf until after school.

When Mama heard about this Tressie got her legs switched good for being sassy to the teacher.

If we got in trouble at school, we had double trouble at home, so the doll's school days were over.

Another time Tressie was called for her spelling lesson and asked to spell "hen." She wouldn't even try, so Miss Ann (Miss Ann Dale had taken Miss McKay's place when she retired) told her if she didn't pay attention and spell her words, she would switch her legs and reached for the switch that she always kept handy on her desk.

Tressie said, "Okay, h-e-n spells hen. Now, how do you spell 'rooster'?" The students all laughed, and so did Miss Ann.

Chapter 24

All the houses had attics where things not in use were kept. In winter, down came the feather beds and double-wool blankets, quilts, and comforters. How nice and warm we slept in those beds. The big stove downstairs was kept burning all night.

In the long evenings Mama read stories to us, taught us Bible lessons, and told us all about her home in Kansas and how one day we would go there and visit her relatives. She said it would be a different world to us.

Other times we would sit around eating popcorn, apples, and hickory nuts. Daddy would sing songs and play the mouth organ, or harp, they called it, or the Jew's harp — a strange-looking little gadget he put to his mouth and hit with his fingers somehow. We were all warm and cozy in our little house.

Mama was afraid to stay at home alone at nighttime, and very seldom had to.

Sometimes some men would come to the village to talk politics, and Uncle Cy and Daddy would go.

I remember one night they planned to go into town and Mama was complaining about staying alone.

Daddy told her to lock the doors and go to sleep. There were no thieves around.

We did go to bed, and much later Mama heard noises out by the chicken pen. Then the hens began squawking.

Mama was too scared to move; she lay there awake until Daddy came home. She told him someone had been taking our chickens. He told her it was a skunk or weasel, maybe, and he didn't go see.

Next morning we found three of our pet hens, Dora, Flora, and Cora, with their feet tied together under the big lilac bush, by the back door.

Mama said, "Yes, there was a two-legged skunk out there, and at least a dozen of my hens are gone."

Daddy bought some more to replace them. We named most of the chickens, and had some pretty little bantams.

We played with the chickens, putting them in the doll buggy and pushing them all around. We dressed our cats up in doll clothes and took them riding, too. They didn't seem to mind. I guess the Humane Society would be after us these days, for cruelty to animals. We never hurt them.

We called our cats Dolly and Polly. They were tomcats, but we didn't know.

I wish my children would have been raised on a farm. It is a great place to start living.

In the fall Uncle Cy told Bonnie and me that he would give us money if we would walk along the fences and pull the wool from the barbed wire where the sheep had rubbed it off.

Bonnie and I took sacks and walked up and down the fences, gathering wool. Then we walked back to the house, where Uncle Cy would give us our money.

We saved it to buy Christmas presents for our families and each other.

The little blue pin tray on my dresser is one Bonnie gave me when we were eight years old. It had pink roses painted on it and gold paint around the edges. This has all faded away now, but I still love it. Bonnie has passed on.

I treasure the memory of that old house on the hill, with all the pretty roses, lilacs, and red clover. We pulled the heads of the clover and dried them in the sun. Mama made sweet-smelling pillows of them.

Chapter 25

One day Grandpa Jeff was taken very ill. There was no one to look after him, so Daddy said it was our duty to move to his home until he was well again.

We cried and didn't want to leave. Daddy told us that no matter where we lived or what happened to anything we possessed, we wouldn't really lose it, that places and memories would always be with us wherever we went. How very true that is, and how nice it is now to remember that old farm.

We moved to Grandpa's home. We missed Bonnie and Jewel, but could see them at church each week and when they came shopping at the general store.

It was nice living at Grandpa's. There weren't many families in Quick City, so we knew them all. Most of them had been there for years.

There was one store and post office combined, a railroad station, two churches (the First Christian and the Baptist), and under the big oak trees was the blacksmith shop.

There was a high bank above the railroad track, where the children would gather to watch the trains go by and to wave at the conductors, brakemen, and engineers. Often they would bring sacks of candy and throw it up on the bank to us as they went by. We seldom missed a train, just in case they did bring the candy.

Then there was the beautiful big lake along one side of the town; they called it Big Creek. It was large like a lake, and everyone fished there.

We liked going to Aunt Oma and Uncle Jim's home. They raised the best tomatoes I've ever tasted, and they would give us the salt shakers and tell us to go help ourselves. We didn't need to be told twice.

Our little brother, Lynn, couldn't get around like the rest of us. The doctors talked of operating, but each time they were ready for the surgery, Mama would stop them.

As he grew older he wanted to go barefooted like the rest of us did. Mama said no, it would hurt his ankle too much. He walked on the anklebone, couldn't turn it over flat and straighten his foot out.

Mama told Dr. Scheaffer and he said, "Let him try it. Maybe he will try to turn his foot over if it hurts him."

So Lynn started leaving his shoes off, and he cured that foot himself. By the time he was twelve years old, he had not even a limp, no more braces or special shoes.

Chapter 26

Extra things needed by the people were brought from Kansas City on the train. Each family had their Sears & Roebuck catalogs. The Sears Company had started in 1887 as a jewelry company selling watches and rings in Chicago.

We also had the Montgomery Ward catalog. Aaron Montgomery Ward started his store in Chicago in a single room over a livery stable in 1872.

We could order most anything we wanted from these mail-order houses. I remember the excitement of waiting for the boxes to come on the train.

How we treasured those great books. Until the new ones came, that is; then the old ones were taken to the outhouses.

Those little houses were kept very clean. Lime was applied often, and benches and floors were scrubbed with the old lye soap.

Here is the recipe for lye soap; in case of a deep depression or recession, you might want to make some. It is hard on the hands, but I know it really does do a good job.

For Hard Soap

Empty the contents of one can of lye into a large iron kettle, containing one quart of water. Stir with a long paddle or stick. The lye will dissolve and become quite hot. Allow to cool. Now take a crock half-full (or five pounds) of clear grease, tallow, or butter, melt until lukewarm. Then commence pouring the cold lye into the melted grease, gradually, until it is thoroughly mixed and drops from the stick or paddle, the thickness of honey. Stir 10 minutes, spread on a long pan. Let set until cold and cut into bars.

See how easy it was?

They also made what was called snow liniment. Here is that recipe.

Snow Liniment

Take 1 cup vinegar, 1 cup turpentine, and 1 raw egg.
Shake well. Will look like cod liver oil. When finished, rub on.

I guess this must have been for frostbite or sore muscles. I have many such recipes in Aunt Cora Belle's old cookbook.

Chapter 27

The church we went to was the Baptist and was just across the street from Grandpa Jeff's home.

As he gained health and strength, he started teaching us our Sunday school lessons. Each Saturday afternoon, come rain or shine, we were gathered together and kept until we knew the Golden Text. We call it memory verse now. We must know our lesson for the next day.

Sunday was the day of rest in Quick City. We had church in the mornings; in the af-

71

ternoons, the people who were sick were visited. Children played quietly; no fishing or ball games were allowed.

The pastor, Brother Davenport, we called him, came from his home in Harrisonville, about twenty-five miles away. He came on the train Saturday evenings and left Monday mornings.

I was always getting into trouble. I forgot children should be seen and not heard. I remembered to say "Yes, sir" and "No, ma'am," to stand up when older people entered the room: things they called manners. I usually spoiled it all by saying what I thought, and I'd suffer the consequences later.

Brother Davenport was having a problem with his teeth, which were yellow colored. One day he was out in the yard, brushing his teeth, and said he wished he could get them to look white, but no matter how much he brushed, it didn't help.

So I said, "Why don't you use some soda? That will take it off."

He said, "Who told you that, Jessie Lee?"

I said, "Oh, we do it all the time."

He told me to go in and ask my mama to send him a little baking soda.

I ran into the house and said, "Give me some soda, quick!"

"What for?" Mama asked.

"He wants to get his teeth white, and I told him to use soda like we do."

Mama said, "Jessie Lee, you didn't."

She gave it to me and I guess he liked it. He always asked for some after that.

One Sunday Aunt Oma was sick, and the family all went to visit her, leaving Tressie and me home to play. We got tired of that and decided to go fishing.

We got the poles and took off across the pasture to the lake. We caught some nice ones and got home about the same time as the folks did.

Then we got a grand scolding for fishing on Sunday. We were feeling real guilty, when Brother Davenport came out and said, "Now, Margaret, don't be too hard on the girls. No real harm done."

He looked at the fish and said, "Let's clean them for breakfast in the morning."

We felt much better after that, but it was still the rule: "No Fishing on Sunday."

We didn't have fancy reels, just lines and hooks tied to a pole with a red bobber that lay on the water until the fish jerked it under. Our bait was grasshoppers and worms.

No greater joy can I imagine than a clean blue sky, a quiet stream, a fishing pole, a good book, and an apple in your pocket.

Chapter 28

Grandpa was well again, and Daddy needed a better job. We couldn't go back to the house on the hill; someone else lived there now. So Daddy got a job with Harry Evans.

Harry and his wife, Leo, had two nice farms close together. They hired Daddy to help with the farming, something he was good at. We moved into a house half a mile beyond the Evans home and on the opposite side of the road.

It was another beautiful farm. The house sat back from the road under two large sugar maple trees, with a large oak tree at the back door. The house was painted white with green trim. Rosebushes and lilacs were scattered over the yard of pretty blue grass. How I loved those yellow roses.

There was a walk made of large rocks from the house to the road. There was a picket fence with a gate; we got scolded for swinging on it.

There wasn't much fruit here, but more than two families could use. We bought more chickens, some pigs, and a cow I was scared to go near. Soon we were very much at home again.

Here is where I first began dreaming my beautiful dreams, the things I'd do when I grew up. I was going to have the most wonderful life, and live in a big house. I'd have a fine carriage and horses and a large family. We would have parties and happy times. First I thought I would be a schoolteacher.

I sat on the seat of an old cultivator that had been placed under a tree in the backyard. I loved to watch the clouds and imagine I saw people, animals, castles, all kinds of things flying around on those fast-moving clouds. I could completely forget where or who I was, until I was called back by my mother's whistle, the one she used to summon us to the house.

Sunday afternoons we took long walks in the woods, along the back side of the farm, and watched rabbits and squirrels.

We would find wildflowers, and sometimes we would see a mother quail with her covey of little ones, taking her family for a walk. She would make a noise and run toward us while the little ones fled into the brush, then away she went. All mothers try to protect their babies.

We found violets, columbines, bluebells, wild roses, and many other flowers scattered all through the woods. There were black-berries, persimmon and hickory nut trees, which we visited when their fruit was ripe.

Mama and Mrs. Evans, or Leo, as she wanted us to call her, soon became good friends. I thought Leo a strange name for a girl. She said her father had wanted a boy, so they gave her a boy's name.

We now went to a different school, called the Bee Branch. I didn't like this school so much, although we did enjoy the walk because there were no hills to climb. The roadside had wild cherries and many hazel-nut bushes. Wild canaries were every place you looked.

I can't remember the teacher's name, or what she was like. The building was about the same as Possum Trot. The boys teased the girls and made them cry.

One boy called John was always trying to kiss us. I didn't like him one bit. One day he grabbed me and I scratched his face good and deep with my fingernails. He never bothered me again, but they called me "the Little Wildcat" after that.

Chapter 29

Now we had our first telephone; it was quite an attraction to Tressie and me. We had seen them, but never had one in our house. Our ring was one long ring and two short rings. One long ring meant Central had news for everyone, and a dash was made to the phone. I had to stand on a stool to reach the receiver. Listening to people talk was a favorite pastime of mine. The telephone was a wonder to Tressie and me, as were the funny papers.

They came each Sunday morning on the early morning train from Kansas City. Uncle Jim saved them for us, and when we went into Quick City, that's the first place we went. Sometimes we got several at one time, if the roads had been bad or Daddy had been too busy to take us for a while.

Mama didn't allow me to listen in on the neighbors' conversations. She said, "Ladies don't eavesdrop."

Well, I wasn't a lady, just a little girl. So I continued my listening habits.

All would be well until I would forget and

mentioned something I couldn't have known without listening on the phone.

Then Mama would say, "Jessie dear, you have been at that phone again."

She always called me "Jessie dear" unless I did something to upset her, then she would call out, "Jessie Lee Brown, you come here this minute." Then she'd ask, "Did you do this or that?" And I would hang my head and say, "Yes, ma'am."

We learned very young it was better to tell the truth than to try to lie to her — she hated lies. I never remember Daddy spanking me or Lynn. Sometimes he had to spank Tressie when she threw a temper fit and was so sassy.

One day I heard the phone ring, and as only Lynn and I were in the room, I rushed to the phone. I knew it was the Johnson family ring.

I heard Mr. Johnson say hello, and a man said, "This is Dr. Greyson in Kansas City and I have some bad news for you. It is about your daughter Marcia Page. She has been shot by her husband, Jack. He then shot himself."

Mr. Johnson said, "Oh, no, my God, no!"

Then he said to Mrs. Johnson, "Marcia and Jack are dead."

I could hear her screaming and crying, "No, no, no!"

Then Mr. Johnson said to the doctor, "I will come there on the next train."

I felt terrible and ran outside to find Mama.

She insisted I had dreamed it. Then she said, "Have you been at that phone again?"

I said, "Yes, ma'am, and it is true. Jack did shoot Marcia and himself, too."

She forgot to scold me and went to the phone. It seemed I hadn't been the only one listening that morning, so she heard all about the tragic event.

I hated bad news and stopped listening in for a long, long time. Mr. Evans had a hired man who was very nice, and he stayed with us while Mama and Daddy went to the funeral.

Seemed the Johnson family had a lot of bad luck. Their little girl Naomi was burned to death that same year. Her clothing caught fire from a fire that had been built in the yard.

She was my age and we were friends. School was dismissed the day of her funeral so the children might attend the funeral, my first.

I have never forgotten it. The little casket was placed in the parlor. Someone was playing the organ softly.

They let us walk by the casket and look at her; her face was burned so much, it didn't look like her at all.

Then they took the children to the back of the room. The preacher stood beside her and talked about seeing her again in heaven.

I decided it wasn't quite so bad if we could find her again in heaven, where I was sure she would be happy. We often talked of heaven and how wonderful it was.

Her death was a big shock to the neighbors. We were told never to light a match or go near an open fire. The matches were in a tin box high up on the kitchen wall, where only Mama or Daddy could reach them.

I liked living on the farm. I could feed the chickens and gather the eggs. I would watch them hatch. First the tiny hole made larger by the little chick until finally it was out of the shell. Beautiful little creatures; I loved them.

Chapter 30

I began to have more chores to do.

Tressie and I had to churn the butter. How we hated that job, standing there splashing that dasher up and down until the cream turned to butter.

One day Mama took some half-gallon fruit jars and put the cream in them. We shook them and rolled them on the floor until it was butter. That was work, too.

Butchering was the time I hated most of all.

If it was done at our place, one or two of the neighbors came to help. The men would kill the poor pigs by sticking a knife in their throat to make them bleed good. Then they dipped them into a very large iron kettle of boiling water and hung them on a pole that had been put up across two large posts and nailed there.

Next they took some kind of a scraper and scraped all the hair off. The pig looked all pink and white and clean then.

They let it hang there awhile, then took it to the smokehouse and cut it up. I never

81

watched this. There would be shoulders, hams, and bacon smoking in hickory smoke for a long time.

Then came the sausage making. The meat was put through a large grinder, then mixed with salt, spices, whatever sausage contains, and put into large stone jars. Lard was melted and poured over it, then covered and put away. Sure was good.

Then the lard was rendered, how I hated that. Always made me sick to smell it.

Whoever helped with the butchering took some of the fresh meat home with them. When Daddy went to help them, he brought some home. Everyone had fresh meat all winter.

Uncle Frank's old sow had a litter of piglets and one was a little runt. He said it was sure to die, as the others wouldn't let it eat.

I begged him to let me take it home with me.

He said all right if F.A. didn't care.

It was Mama I had to worry about. She thought we had enough to do without that pig to hand feed.

I promised to do that, so at last she said all right.

It grew nicely, and the larger it became, the bigger nuisance it was. It was fun when it was little, to have it follow us around the farm, but not so funny as it grew up. It got dangerous to go outside, and it seemed that pig could always find a way out of his pen.

Mama was afraid he would cause someone to have a bad fall. She said he had to go, so poor Porky was taken away.

Tressie, Lynn, and I cried our bucket of tears, though it didn't do any good. I imagine we ate him that winter.

We built playhouses under the trees. We made mud pies and cakes, put weeds in old cans, covered them with water, and that was our canned fruit. Couldn't imagine why we soon had to throw them far away — because of the smell, I guess. That old black mud made the prettiest cakes and pies.

I would dream on of all the nice things I would do when I got big. I was going to be a good cook, learn to sew, so many things. Oh, the mind of a little girl . . . the dreams and the hopes they have.

Chapter 31

Mama did sewing for many of the friends and neighbors.

One woman I'll call Aunt Nellie had six children, two girls and four boys. We didn't like them to come to our house, because they broke our toys and hit us every chance they got.

Their mother would say, "You children play nice now." They never did. They tore up our playhouse, and I was always afraid they would find my dolls. I hid them when I saw them coming.

I had twenty-three dolls and spent a lot of time with them. I had a place I loved to go to be by myself. It was in the big tree by the kitchen door. Daddy built me a little platform and put a fence around it so I wouldn't fall. I spent some time there on all nice days. Lynn couldn't climb because of his foot, and Tressie was too fat at that time.

One day Mama was tired out from all the sewing she had been doing, with everyone getting ready for school. She said, "I hope no one comes today."

About ten o'clock Mama looked out the door and said, "Oh my, here comes Aunt Nellie with those ornery kids." We ran to hide our most prized possessions.

Mama told us to play in the backyard, she had a headache. We went gladly — anything to keep them outside.

Mama measured and pinned Aunt Nellie's clothes like she wanted them. Soon it was dinnertime. Mama got that on the table, then went to lie down.

After eating, we children ran outside to play. I got tired of their games and climbed my tree.

After eating, Aunt Nellie said they would have to go home, Uncle Ned had gone to Kansas City early that morning and would come back on the evening freight train. It came through Quick City about four P.M.

I thought maybe Aunt Nellie would do the dishes this time, but no — not Aunt Nellie. She came out and called, "Jessie Lee, come in and do these dishes, your poor mama is so tired."

I didn't answer. She came back and didn't see me in the tree. When she finally found me she said, "Jessie Lee, aren't you ashamed of yourself? Don't you feel sorry for your poor mama?"

"No," I said, "I won't come down and you can't make me. My poor mama wouldn't be so tired if you didn't bring your kids here for dinner so much. And we wouldn't have so many dishes to wash."

She flew into the house to tell Mama what a horrid child I was, then she gathered her tribe and went home.

Mama came out and called, "Jessie Lee Brown, come down here right now. I am ashamed of you, talking to a guest like that!"

I was to go to my room and stay there, she would deal with me later. I came down from my tree in a hurry. It didn't pay not to mind Mama.

Later, of course, I did do the dishes and got a lecture on how ladies didn't act like that. I was sure I would get switched, but I guess Mama's head ached too badly.

I had to stand on a wooden box to be able to reach the dishpan on the kitchen cabinet. We had no sink or no running water. Mama fixed the dishwater for me, a pan to rinse them in, and a rack to put them on.

Below the tabletop were drawers: one for flour, one for bread, and smaller ones for silverware and small items. We also had a large pantry.

My work beside the dishes was clearing the table and carrying the dishes to the kitchen, and be careful not to soil the tablecloth. Mama didn't like oilcloth on her table.

We had an old wash machine; Tressie and I took turns pushing that old wooden handle back and forth on. Mama thought it was great. Me? No comment.

Chapter 32

That winter was very cold. The Johnson family got the scarlet fever. Neighbors went to help care for the children. One of the little boys died.

Mama always worked too hard for the strength she had. She and I both had malaria fever every few months. Mama went night after night to help the sick neighbors.

Then Lynn got the scarlet fever and was very sick. Tressie and I had already had it in Washington. We were quarantined.

After Lynn got well and we were fumigated, and back in school, Mama got sick again. What a winter. . . .

It was near Christmastime. We always

had a pretty tree, which we decorated. We strung popcorn and cranberries on chains, took strips of bright colored paper and pasted them together to form chains and draped them over the tree. We had a pretty angel for the top branch.

To us it was wonderful. We would hang up our stockings of netting, made for the occasion. They would be filled with small surprises, oranges, hard candy, and nuts.

This year Mama called us to come and listen carefully to what she said. She told us that because she was sick, and the snow was so deep, she didn't think we would have our usual Christmas, that Santa Claus might not get to all the homes because of the bad weather. Maybe Daddy would find a nice tree and we could decorate it. Daddy said we could count on that for sure.

We were going to have a program at the school, and Santa was supposed to be there. I wondered how he could get to the schoolhouse but not to ours. I kept still for once.

The days passed quickly. The school program was to be Friday afternoon, and the parents would be there. Mama was still sick, so Daddy had to stay with her.

The snow was still there. Some of the neighbors came and helped us with our Christmas tree, which Daddy had managed to find and bring home.

I was worried for sure now. Who would cook Christmas dinner? Mama always made English plum pudding, a lot of pies, cakes, and cookies. This year she had to stay in bed.

Friday morning came bright and clear. Again Mama told Tressie and me not to be too disappointed if Santa didn't have anything for us. Maybe he hadn't received our letters. We were to be brave and not cry.

One of the neighbors came by and took Tressie and me to the school on a big bobsled. Each child recited a little poem or sang a song. Then everyone sang Christmas carols. The parents seemed to enjoy that very much.

At last our teacher said, "Well, children, it is time for us to see what Santa Claus has for you."

She opened the door and in came Santa Claus. He was a fat man with white whiskers and a bright red suit, and he was carrying a very large sack over his shoulder.

He had a happy voice, calling greetings to us as he took his place beside the Christmas tree. He said, "I hope you have all been good boys and girls this year."

I thought, If we don't get anything, everyone will think we have been real bad.

Santa started calling names. The child would go to the tree and Santa would say a few words to them and hand them a gift.

At last the big surprise came. He called out, "Jessie Lee and Teresa Brown, here is something for you."

I don't know how I ever walked up there, thanked him, and got back to my seat. I know I was trembling like a leaf, trying not to cry.

I was all thumbs opening that package. At last there it was, a beautiful little signet ring with a "J" on it. Teresa's was the same, only with a "T" on hers.

I don't ever remember being so happy at a school Christmas party as we were that day. We thanked old Santa over and over again.

Each child received a long net stocking filled to the top with oranges, nuts, and candy. What a happy ending to a day we had dreaded so much.

When we got home, Mama was as surprised as we were.

Long after that we learned that Leo Evans had managed to get to Kansas City and bought the rings for us. She was a dear woman who loved children. She had none of her own.

Christmas Eve we went to bed early. I

had faith now that there would be something nice under that tree.

Later we heard people coming in and a lot of talking, but we were used to neighbors coming to visit. This year, they had all brought something nice for our Christmas dinner.

Next morning when we got up there were packages under that tree. Daddy had managed to get to Blairtown, ten miles away, and get something for all.

We had a rule: No presents until after breakfast. How we hurried to get dressed and eat! Then the excitement.

When I think of you, my grandchildren, and the lovely things you get each year, I guess you would be plenty disappointed with this Christmas of ours. Tressie and I had high-top shoes with little red tassels at the top, some pretty colored beads, and material for a new dress. Tressie got a ball, too. She always wanted to play ball. Lynn got a spinning top, bright red, and a little iron train. It was my best Christmas.

Chapter 33

A few days later Mama's brother, Uncle Walter, came and took over. He had cooked in a restaurant for years and could fix a meal in no time.

Mama started getting better. Maybe Uncle Walt with his news from her home helped her.

Uncle Walt liked to go hunting; he would get rabbits, squirrels, whatever was to be hunted at that time of year. He used to dress, or clean, the rabbits and squirrels and hang them out on the clotheslines to freeze.

We were sorry when Uncle Walt's vacation ended and he had to return to Manhattan. He had brightened our lives a lot.

Now spring was coming again, with its blessings giving hope to all, after that long, cold winter. Just as it always has down through the ages. . . .

Still, Mama didn't get as strong as she should, so Daddy decided to leave the farm and move back to Quick City. We found a nice house in the center of the village. (I visited it in 1946; it has been modernized now.)

Across from us lived Aunt Mell Higgins, our uncle Bert's mother. She had four children: Uncle Bert, Otto, Pearl, and Meryl. Otto and Pearl were teenagers; Meryl was about twelve. They were fine neighbors.

Daddy went to work for the railroad. We liked living near the church and Grandpa again. He was such a nice person. He had thick white hair (so pretty) and a long beard. He kept it neat and clean.

He took us fishing and would see that our Sunday school lessons were learned once again. We had missed not being able to go to the church every Sunday while on the farm. Mama had taught us our lessons at home. Grandpa Jeff was the Sunday school superintendent and loved every minute of his church work.

There were many more things to do in the village. Church socials were held in the churchyards. There was a big Fourth of July celebration and so on.

One time for the July Fourth celebration we went to Sulphur Springs, Missouri. Some of our relatives and neighbors went too.

We took a lot of food and started before the sun was up and stayed for the fireworks. They weren't like the ones of modern days; there was more noise, as I remember it.

They claimed the water from those springs was good for your health and gave us some to drink. The smell was terrible and the taste was worse. I decided that I would rather be sick than drink that water.

All the grown-ups were busy visiting, so the children just wandered around looking to see all we could. There were lots of flags, and firecrackers going off in all directions. Later some men talked about our country, and everyone sang songs.

It was a tired group of people when we reached home that night, or perhaps it was the next morning.

Another thing Tressie and I liked very much were the revival meetings, held under huge tents once or twice a year.

Everyone went. The singing was wonderful. Tressie and I joined in and learned many beautiful old hymns there.

The ministers told us of the missionary work being done. I decided I had better be a missionary instead of a schoolteacher, and go away to other lands. Very nice dreams. . . .

When the meetings were over, usually on a Sunday afternoon, all the people who had repented their sins and wanted to join one of the churches marched down to the lake to be baptized.

We would all go and watch. The preacher would wade out to the right spot. Then one at a time, the people walked slowly to meet him. He would say a few words, place a handkerchief in their hand, place the hand over their mouth, then dip them under the water.

I worried every time that he would drop one of them, and they would drown. But he never did. I watched Mama and Daddy both baptized in that lake.

As the people came back, dripping wet, someone would wrap a blanket around them, and soon all would be home again.

It seemed rather foolish to me at that time. I didn't understand. Those people drove miles to get to church on Sundays. Now so many are too indifferent to even go a few blocks.

Saturday afternoons there were ball games in the large pasture by our house. Teams came from many of the small towns — Harrisonville, Holden, Latour — and the people enjoyed the games played there as much as they now enjoy the ones in the great ball parks.

We had no bands, no baton-twirling girls with scanty uniforms. In fact, if girls had dared to come out in public dressed — or undressed — like those of today, they would have been hurried away to jail.

A box was passed around the crowd and money collected to buy new baseballs, bats, and caps.

Chapter 34

I mustn't forget to tell you about the family who came from Tennessee, the Hixsons and the Stills. Will and Julia Still were the grandparents. Manda, their daughter, was married to Charlie Hixson. Their children were Claude, Stella, and Eula.

The men drove their wagons there from Tennessee. The rest came on the train. It was their first train ride.

We had no hotel, so they had to stay around with neighbors until they found a house. They found one next to Grandpa Jeff's home; it was behind the First Christian Church.

Tressie and I were anxious to go visit them, but Mama always wanted to wait until she knew more about people before getting too friendly. If they were what she called "nice people," then we could visit all we wanted. She soon found out that they were very nice, kind people and they went to the Baptist church, so from then on we were all pals.

Mama had strict rules about people. She said it paid to go slow getting acquainted with strangers because you were judged by the company you kept, and your reputation was your most valued possession.

We called the Stills Uncle Will and Aunt Julie, and the Hixsons Uncle Charlie and Aunt Mandy. Aunt Julie could tell the best ghost stories, and she believed them, too. She told us stories about the war and how the damn Yankees stole everything they had, how they hid the cornpone and cold sweet potatoes in the baby's cradle so they had something to eat — and all sorts of things, until I was sure a Yankee was a monster and I hoped I would never meet up with one of them. I would listen spellbound to her tell of Tennessee and how it used to be.

Aunt Julie and Aunt Mandy made the best sour milk biscuits I have ever eaten. To this day I haven't seen any like them. Not even Mama's.

In an old shed in back of their house they had an old wooden loom for weaving carpets. We loved to watch them weave.

They took large balls of rags that had

been cut into inchwide strips and sewed together, and then with a large wooden shuttle Aunt Julie would weave it through the strings, or carpet warp, that were fastened from the top of the machine, or loom, as they called it. It was strung up like the strings on a fiddle. She wove that shuttle through those strings, then pulled on a wooden bar and pushed a pedal with her feet. This made the rags fit close together and look pretty.

Mama decided we needed a new carpet for the parlor. (A parlor is what we now call the living room, or where company was entertained.) Children seldom entered that room.

Mama decided I was old enough to learn to sew rags. I learned fast and liked it. They were hard to wind into large balls, and it took a lot of them to make a carpet.

Mama inspected my sewing often to be sure I was fastening the thread good. She didn't want that carpet coming apart. When the neighbor ladies came to visit they would help us sew rags.

Chapter 35

Aunt Cora Belle and Uncle Bert and Lillie, Clyde, and Bob Moore all decided to leave Washington and move back to Missouri. Lillie and Bob had another little boy now, Scott. (He lives with his wife in California. I had a letter from them today.)

I never knew why they left Washington. Maybe to be with Grandpa Jeff — he was getting old, and Uncle Bert's mother wasn't well. We were glad to have them near again.

Aunt Dora Lee and Uncle Frank lived on a farm and didn't come to our home often. They had two more children, Egonda and Angus.

I liked to go to their home; sometimes Tressie and I got to go home with them for a few days. We would roam all over that farm.

Aunt Dora Lee was a very pretty woman, with very blue eyes and light brown hair and what Mama said was a peaches-and-cream complexion. I asked if that was nice and she said, *Very.*

She was always busy, so she didn't talk

99

to us as much as Aunt Cora Belle did. Still, I liked Dora Lee very much. She was kind and told us stories at bedtime, and heard our prayers and tucked us in with a little kiss. There wasn't much rest time for mothers on farms.

Aunt Cora Belle and Uncle Bert always had time for us all. After they came back from Washington they lived with Grandpa, and she fixed the place up so nice. I loved to go there. Aunt Cora Belle had so many pretty pictures and seashells and pretty pillows, crocheted doilies, and rugs. The pillows were covered with velvet or woolens with cross-stitch and feather stitching on them. She taught me to do the simple stitches. It was hard to learn to sew from Mama; she was left-handed. So was brother Lynn.

Aunt Cora Belle was about five feet six inches tall and had beautiful dark brown eyes like Daddy and Tressie. She had a lovely complexion that lasted all her life. She lived to be ninety-four years old. Some of my nicest memories are of her and Uncle Bert.

She didn't care much for visiting like lots of the ladies did. She said she didn't enjoy their idle gossip, asking questions that were none of their business or talking about everyone else. She would help out when someone was sick, play the organ on Sundays, and help with the ice-cream socials on the church lawns.

When they had those parties, the ladies all brought cakes and brought their ice-cream freezers and whatever went into them. The men went to the icehouse, where the ice was kept packed in sawdust. They would bring it up and pack the freezers full and turn the handle until the ice cream was done.

Lanterns were hung around in trees or set on tables made of long boards put across

Jessie Lee's father, Flemington Almer Brown (center) with sisters Cora Belle (left) and Dora Lee, and parents Mary Elizabeth and John Jefferson Brown.

sawhorses or barrels. They carried chairs from the nearby homes.

Everyone was happy and having fun.

In winter they had oyster soup suppers in a large room over the store. All this was to raise money for the church.

It didn't cost so much to keep our church going. It was done the easy way, everyone doing their share. No one charged for their services. Our organ sounded beautiful, and the people sang like they really meant it. Each family gave money for the pastor.

Chapter 36

At our house we had one room we didn't use. In the fall, quilting frames were put up in there. When the quilt tops were pieced and sewed together, they were lined with flour sacks or muslin.

Everyone had plenty of flour sacks because each family baked their own bread, biscuits, cakes, and cookies. (No bakeries. . . .) The flour sacks were used to make sheets, pillows, pillowcases, tablecloths, underwear, and many other things.

After the quilt was basted together, it was

fastened to the frames and a pattern stitched into it with tiny stitches. There were many patterns for quilts — the necktie, wedding ring, big star, far too many to mention.

Anyone having time would come by and quilt awhile. By the time that one was done, someone else would have one ready. So it went, on and on, helping one another and having fun too.

All children liked these days when the mamas sewed, quilted, or sewed rags for carpets. We could play in the churchyard under the big oak and maple trees. Some of the fathers had put up some nice swings for us, and along one side of the churchyard was a long row of iron posts with heavy iron chains forming a fence where people tied their horses on Sundays. We played skin the cat on that chain.

Sometimes we all went to Aunt Cynthy's farm. There was a lot of room to play there. She had quilting parties too.

Tressie and I got to go with Aunt Cora Belle and Uncle Bert when they went to Blairstown or Holden to shop. We enjoyed these trips very much. We would come home with material for new dresses, and almost always I would get more pretty colored beads. I loved the little rings that came on sticks of peppermint candy. Mama used to say, "Jessie Lee, I think there must have been a Gypsy in your ancestry someplace." I guarded my treasures in a pretty box.

Some of the ladies didn't like Aunt Cora Belle because she didn't like to gossip with them. She said, "People who were brought up right don't go snooping around into other people's business." She said she could tell a lot about a person just listening to them talk a few minutes.

She wore white blouses or shirtwaists, they were called, and long dark skirts. She had a gold watch on a long chain she wore over her heart, fastened with a pretty pin with colored sets in it. I thought it was so beautiful, and planned to get one like it when I grew up. Seemed a long time it was taking.

There were so many things to learn, like the things to respect, like our flag and the president, and the White House where he lived. Daddy said if you didn't like the way the president did things, to just be quiet and vote for someone else next time, but as long as he remained in office, he was to be respected. He was the people's choice.

Then there were the old people; you must never talk back to them, and be quiet when they were talking. We were to mind our teachers; if we didn't, we would get the switch.

Then there were the bad sins to remember — not to cheat, tell lies or steal, or swear, or use any bad words or listen to bad stories. Mama said that was filling your mind up with trash when there were so many worthwhile things to be stored away there.

All that was a lot to remember.

When little girls went outdoors in the summertime, we had to wear sunbonnets. Oh, they were pretty, but so uncomfortable, starched stiff as a board. We were told it was to keep us from getting freckles and sunburn. We would have preferred the freckles. Our dresses were starched stiff, too.

Everything was ironed. I started ironing the small items when I was seven. We had old flat irons, heated on top of the stove. They were made of iron, and many burned hands resulted from not getting the thick pad on the handle just right.

That old basket would be full of starched clothes. The night before ironing day Mama took water and sprinkled the clothes, rolled them tight, and covered the basket. Early next morning she started ironing.

Monday was washday, Tuesday was ironing day, Wednesday baking day. Mama baked bread again on Saturday and cinnamon rolls, doughnuts, or cookies. No wonder so many women died so young.

Chapter 37

When we had colds we had to stay home from school and take cold remedies.

Mama would bring the washtub in by the fire, put warm water in it, and give us a bath. Then she would put us into long flannel nightgowns after rubbing our chests with goose grease that had turpentine and kerosene mixed in it. She gave us cough syrup made of boiled onions and sugar, or cough syrup made in Kansas City of rock candy and whiskey. I liked the one Mama made better. She never made us wear the little sacks of asafetida on a string around our neck like some mamas did.

I don't know how the poor teachers stood those horrid smells they had to deal with through the winter term. I don't know if it was the medicines or the smell of them that cured us, but we lived and grew nicely.

The snow used to get so deep that it covered the fence posts, then froze solid, like the ice on the lake. We would walk over it to school. This school wasn't nearly so far from our home as the others had been.

Last year I talked to a man at the bus station in Springfield, Missouri (we were snowbound there). We were talking of the old days in Missouri, and I told him how we had walked over the deep snow to school and he said he had, too. But no more. A few inches of snow paralyzes a city these days. (Dean, Don, Dan, and David, my Minnesota Vikings, I can't tell you much about snow, can I?)

Chapter 38

By the time I was ten years old, I was reading everything I could find. Mama and her cousin Hattie got books from Holden and Kansas City. After they finished reading them, they put them in a box in the attic. It was easy for me to get them.

I would slip upstairs into the attic and read. Of course I didn't understand all I read, and many words were beyond me, but I enjoyed reading what I could of them. When

Mama discovered what I was reading, she said, "Those books are not for little girls," and they moved them to Hattie's attic.

Mama and cousin Hattie had their beauty secrets, too. They put buttermilk and some stuff they got in Kansas City on their faces. They had some powder that smelled nice they put on their faces when they went someplace. They also bought corsets "to make their clothes fit better," they said. Mama was too thin and cousin Hattie too fat.

One day I found some red crepe paper and learned that it faded when wet. I proceeded to dampen it and rub it on my face. Then I got some flour from the pantry and put that over the pretty red.

I went to show the kids how fine I looked. They stared at me like I was from outer space. I felt hurt; I thought I looked real pretty.

Later my face began to burn and itch like crazy, and I ran to find Mama.

She said, "Whatever is that on your face?"

I told her and she got the bottle of olive oil and some cotton and cleaned me up.

She asked, "What on earth did you do that for?" and I told her I wanted to be pretty.

My face was a mess; it broke out with a

rash and was some time clearing.

Later I heard Mama and cousin Hattie talking about it.

Hattie said, "I suppose she was trying to imitate us, but if we had that little minx's complexion, we wouldn't have to try for one in a jar."

Mama said, "No, she takes after her father's side of the family."

Hattie said, "Yes, have you noticed how much like Cora Belle she is?"

I thought that was nice. I liked my auntie and thought she was the nicest person I knew. She was always so neat and clean looking. I wondered, though, what a complexion was and if it was good or bad.

Aunt Dora Lee was very nice too. I didn't know her so well. When they came to our house it was usually in the winter at Christmas holidays. She now had five children: Floyd, Egonda, Angus, Lillian, and Frances. It made a full house and lots of noise when they came.

I always hid my dolls in the attic when they came so they wouldn't get broken. I didn't want anything after it was damaged.

We had lots of fun playing together and lots of good food. Mama and Aunt Dora Lee would cook most of the time.

We had a small room at the back of the

house filled with stone jars of goodies like crocks of milk and butter. At breakfast time they would fry bread dough in bacon grease and brown sugar in a deep iron skillet. They were called stickeys and really were. They were messy to eat, but so good.

Mama used a starter made with water potatoes had been boiled in, some yeast, sugar, and salt. (I haven't made a starter for so long, I have forgotten how.) Sometimes it would go flat; then she borrowed some from a neighbor.

When we came from school in the evening there would be beans and ham cooked in the big iron kettle, cornbread with lots of good butter, milk, and fruit, or the vegetable soup we all liked so much.

Oh, those wonderful smells from that old kitchen with the pretty curtains at the windows and the braided or crocheted rag rugs on the floor. It was home. We were safe from all harm there.

Daddy would dig a big hole in the backyard and put potatoes, turnips, cabbage, onions, and carrots in it, cover them with straw and dirt, and put boards over that and a lot more dirt on top of that. We had them to use until the next crop was ready. That probably isn't exactly the way he did it, but that's how I remember it.

Chapter 39

We always had programs at the church at Christmastime, Mother's Day, and Easter. We learned songs and poems. If we got through our bit without forgetting part of it, we were proud of ourselves. If we forgot, we were so ashamed.

One I had to say it seemed I would never learn, but on Mother's Day I walked up onto the platform (my knees felt like rubber), and in a singsong voice I recited this little poem, which I have never forgotten.

My Mother Says

My mother says she doesn't care
About the color of my hair,
Or if my eyes are blue or brown,
Or if my nose turns up or down.
It really doesn't matter.

My mother says she doesn't care
If I am dark or I am fair,
Or if I'm thin or if I'm fat.

She doesn't fret o'er things like that.
It really doesn't matter.

But if I cheat or tell a lie
Or do mean things to make folks cry,
And do not try to do what is right,
Then that does really matter.

It isn't looks that makes one great,
But character that seals your fate.
It is what's in your heart, you see,
That makes or mars your destiny,
And that does really matter.

(I don't know who wrote these lines, but to say them is like listening to Mama again.)

I stumbled back to my seat. Of course, all the parents applauded when we finished, and I am sure no movie star ever felt more important than I did that day.

At school we had a ball team and played every noontime. We swallowed our lunches as fast as we could so we would have as much time as possible. I couldn't hit the broad side of a barn, but I could really run fast, so they would let someone else bat the ball and me do the running around the bases.

Most students were boys. I liked them

better than the girls. Seemed they were easier to get along with. They weren't always asking silly questions or talking about someone.

Chapter 40

Best of all I liked to go fishing. My cousin Clyde Moore would go with me.

He was a year younger than I was, but a lot larger. He was always doing nice things for me, like baiting my fish hooks, climbing the trees to get me the nicest fruit, and any game I liked to play, so did Clyde.

Sometimes I went fishing alone, and I could bait that hook as fast as anyone, I just didn't like to do it.

Grandpa Jeff was a good fisherman and often took Tressie and me with him. Lynn didn't seem to like to go those days, but he made up for it when he was older. Grandpa taught us how to find the best places to fish.

Aunt Meg Fort often took us with her. We would walk along the railroad track until we came to a nice pond, maybe half a mile away or more. It was so nice and quiet with only the big old bullfrogs croaking away. The water lilies grew there and many fish lived in the water. We usually got several to take home.

Sometimes Aunt Meg would see me headed for the lake with my fishing pole and tell Mama she had seen "little Jeff" going to the lake. Mama would say, "Yes, I don't know what that child will do when we leave here." Mama always planned to come back to Kansas.

Aunt Meg used to tell me about my grandmother Mary Elizabeth, how she had stayed with her husband, Mr. Fort, when he was so sick many nights and how after he died she had gone home so tired, she went to bed and never woke up again. Aunt Meg would say, "An angel she was. Always helping someone." I wish I could have known her.

Well, I thought maybe Grandma would be flying around watching us and we better be good so she wouldn't be ashamed of us. Aunt Meg said you couldn't see angels, but I had seen pictures of them on the little cards they gave us at Sunday school and I thought that someone had to see them to make those pictures.

One evening Daddy said he was going to the lake to fish by moonlight, and Tressie and I could go if we wanted to. Of course we did.

He said we would have to be quiet, that the fish wouldn't bite if it was noisy. It was almost as light as day, and that old moon shining on the water was beautiful. We could see the trees reflected in the water. It was all so quiet and peaceful there.

Daddy had caught several nice ones, and I had a small one. I got a bite and jerked the line out of the water too fast. The hook came sailing out of the water and caught in the lobe of Tressie's ear.

That ended the fishing for that night. We hurried home to get some salve to put on Tressie's ear. I was forbidden to go fishing for a week, so I would remember to be more careful.

There was an old foundation where a house had burned. It had water in the hole and big crawdads lived there. Clyde and I would go fishing for them. The tails made good fish bait. Some folks fried and ate them, but we never did.

We bent pins or pieces of wire and tied that to a piece of string, got a long stick, and tied the string to that. Then we lay on our stomachs and caught those crawdads.

It took a lot of patience to get them out of that hole. Usually, when you got them almost to the edge they let go and fell back in.

We put them in a bucket of water. If we didn't need bait when we got tired of catching them, we dumped them back into the hole until we took a notion to catch them again.

Chapter 41

Tressie spent most of her time with Eula Hixon. They were the same age and played well together. There weren't many children living in Quick City; most families lived on farms. Tressie and Eula are still friends.

I was getting taller and still skinny as a rail. Mama had stopped curling my hair, it was so long. Now she put it in braids that came to my knees and was tied partway down with ribbons that matched my dress.

The kids thought it was fun to give my braids a yank every chance they got, and tied them to the inkwells at school. Each desk had one built into the top.

I often wished I were a boy so I could have short hair. Never dreamed I would live to see the day I couldn't be sure if I'd seen a boy or a girl walking down the street.

Someone gave us a little black-and-tan terrier dog. We named him Dandy. He was the first dog we had owned since Shep in Washington. He went every place we did. When we heard the trains coming, someone would grab Dandy so he wouldn't run on the tracks. We had to be there to see if the men brought the candy. Mama didn't think we should have much candy. But she did make taffy for us when she had time.

Everyone charged their groceries at the village store and paid on payday, once a week or once a month. We were always glad when payday came, because the grocery man sent us a bag of candy.

Aunt Cora Belle and Uncle Bert bought a farm over on Bear Creek. We missed them so much and were so happy when they came to see us. They had a horse and buggy and a little colt that ran along behind its mother. We liked that baby horse, as we called it.

Chapter 42

One morning, as Grandpa was chopping wood for kindling his fires, a piece flew up and hit him in the eye, and it had to be removed. He wore a black patch over it. He went to live with his sister Janette Elliott near Latour, Missouri, until he was well. He never came home again. He died that winter.

They had his funeral at Aunt Janette's home. Relatives and friends came from far and near over those hard frozen roads. He was buried in Rose Hill Cemetery beside Grandma Mary Elizabeth.

Grandpa had told the family to give me his old organ. I had always liked it so much. I liked the fancy carving and the little shelves for candles. I wanted to learn to play it.

Mama hired a girl to give me lessons. Mama sewed for her to pay for the lessons. She came two or three times, collected her new dresses, then ran off and got married.

So ended my musical career. Just as well; I didn't have any talent for it.

Aunt Cora Belle played by ear, and it sounded good to us. She could still play her organ at age ninety-four before she died. She played hymns for me when I visited her in 1963.

Tressie learned to play by ear also.

I don't have to tell you how well your uncle Chick plays. He started at age four with "When the Red, Red Robin Comes Bob, Bob, Bobbin' Along" and nearly drove us crazy with it. Then on to anything he heard and liked; he could learn to play it just by listening and still does.

I think I have enjoyed music as much as, if not better than, anything through my life — all kinds except rock. I draw the line there.

I do hope when I have left this world you will divide my records among you and take care of them. You may be surprised at what you will find. (I love them.) There is Dean Martin at his best, Liberace, Fred Waring, Lawrence Welk, Guy Lombardo, old country music of all kinds. There is also the fine music of the old masters.

I can hear some of you laughing now, saying "Granny and her ideas of music." Well, wait until you play my gospel hymns. I have good music that will live forever, so don't destroy those albums, please.

Don't throw away all my scrapbooks without looking through them. May surprise you, what you might find between the covers of those old books.

I don't throw much away because sooner or later, someone will come along and need the very article you decided was of no use. There is entirely too much careless flinging aside of anything not needed at the moment.

And my books, please don't burn them. Give them to someone who will want them.

Chapter 43

Mama always preached cleanliness, said it was next to godliness. She wanted everything spick-and-span and in its proper place.

I hated making beds and sometimes did a poor job. When she saw it, she made me start all over again and do it right. She would say, "Anything worth doing at all is worth doing right."

We had two families move to the village who sure didn't keep anything neat and clean.

One woman was very fat. She had a boy, Jim, and a girl, Jane, about our ages. They lived at the edge of town. Mama sewed their school clothes.

One day the lady insisted we all come and spend the day. Mama decided we should go.

I remember that she was having chicken and green beans for dinner; the children were getting them ready. They bit the ends off of the beans with their teeth.

That house looked like an insult to pigs. When at last we sat down to eat, it all looked so messy, and the chicken still had feathers on it. So we skinned the meat and ate that. Brother Lynn found a long black hair in his plate. We sat there like wooden Indians, drinking water from cloudy glasses, until we could be excused.

The lady asked why we didn't eat, and Mama said we had had a late breakfast and she guessed we just weren't hungry. That wasn't true, we just couldn't eat that food.

My brother said later, "I won't go back there anymore. She is an old fat lubber of a hair cooker." We never did go back there to eat.

Then there were the Badsleys (I made that name up). I think they lived on eggs. Sarah and Ada, the girls, were skinny like me, and they were so freckled they looked almost brown. They had red hair that looked like it was never combed or washed. Their little brother ran around naked most of the time. He was about two years old.

The girls came to school with eggs on their faces and dirty clothes. Teacher would make them wash up before school started. She kept a basin and some clean clothes in case of need — someone was always getting into a fight or having a nosebleed. (Some of the older boys should have been professionals, they fought so well.)

Sarah and Ada played by themselves most of the time and didn't talk much. Mama told us, Tressie and me, to walk to school with them and be nice. If she ever heard of us teasing them, or making fun of anything they did, she would punish us, and we knew she would keep her word.

Sometimes when we didn't do our work right, Mama would say, "All right, I'll send you to live with the Badsleys." We would shape up in a hurry.

One time, someone bought a bucket, some soap, and a broom and took them to Mrs. Badsley's house with a note saying: "Use these. Cleanliness is next to godliness." They left everything on the porch.

Next day when Mrs. Badsley found them,

she took them inside and didn't even get mad.

Mama said it wasn't a nice thing to do, and she doubted if the poor soul could even read. She reminded us again to be nice to those children.

Cousin Hattie said she knew who did it, but she wouldn't tell.

One thing Mama hated was that some of the women chewed tobacco and dipped snuff. I have heard Daddy say that old Aunt Clara could spit so good she could hit a cat's eye every time. I never saw her try, and I don't know whose aunt she was. Not ours.

Chapter 44

After Grandpa was gone, Daddy decided we should visit Mama's folks in Manhattan, Kansas. We got ready for the trip, a great adventure for us. Mama was so excited to be going home again.

It had rained a lot that year and the old Missouri River was flooding. We started in the afternoon on the train. Only sixty-five miles till we got to Kansas City.

I remember looking out the window and seeing all that water; sometimes it covered the tracks. The train moved very slowly. It began to get dark, and that was really scary.

At last we reached Kansas City, and we were thankful to be there. We went into the depot to wait for a train to Manhattan. Because of the high water, all the trains were late.

Tressie, Lynn, and I had never seen such a busy place. People were rushing around or sitting on benches half-asleep. Men with red caps were carrying baggage.

I liked watching them, until a man walked in the door, looked around in all directions, then walked over to another man, talked to him for a minute or two, then *Bang!* shot him. As he fell to the floor, the man with the gun quietly turned and walked out the side door.

Close by, where we were sitting, everyone seemed paralyzed. Not a sound.

Soon some men came with a sheet or blanket and covered the dead man's body, picked him up, and took him outside. Two more men came with buckets of water and big mops and scrubbed the blood up from the floor.

It was all done and over with so fast that most people probably didn't know what happened. I wanted to ask questions, but was told to be quiet, our train was coming.

We climbed aboard and were soon on our way again. There was still plenty of water wherever we looked.

That was the first violence I had ever witnessed, and the look of surprise and terror on that poor man's face as he fell to the floor I remembered for a long, long time. I have taken many trips since, but that one was by far the most exciting.

At last we arrived at the Union Pacific Depot, and Grandpa was there to meet us. I really felt lost. After our tiny village, this seemed like a very large city. We had been to Holden, Warrensburg, Blairstown, Harrisonville, Latour, but no place like this.

Of course there were no paved streets. They had some brick sidewalks and were working on Poyntz Avenue, paving it with bricks, I think.

This was the first time we had seen Grandma Mary Ellen and Grandpa Milton, or Milt, as people called him. We met Mama's sisters for the first time, and Uncle Jesse.

I had an Aunt Florence, six years older than I. There were Aunt Daisy and Uncle Bert Frost and their two boys, Lyle and Vern. There were Aunt Carrie and Uncle

Roy Lowe and their daughter Mary. We also met Aunt Rose and Uncle Ed Creviston and their four children: Earl, Pearl, Walter, and Olive. There were Aunt Louise and Uncle John Hunter, whose children were Florence, Lois, Scott, Georgia, Donald, and Ruth. There was also Aunt Janette.

That's a lot of people to get acquainted with in two weeks. Cousin Florence was three months other than I and Olive was six months younger, so we were soon friends.

Mama was happy to be with family and friends, but Daddy, Tressie, and I felt a little left out of things and were glad when the time came to go back to Quick City.

Anyway, I was miserable. I had gotten into some poison ivy someplace and I was a sight to behold. My eyes and face were all swollen, and my hands and arms were a mass of blisters. Mama put sugar of lead on me to kill it. It was very poisonous, so I had to be careful about getting it near my mouth. I can still smell that stuff. Thank the Lord for modern remedies.

Going home on the train, I got sick. The malaria was coming back. I hoped I would never have to get on a train again. The water had gone down, and now it was mud all the way, and that mud was *black*.

Mama had enjoyed her visit so much. After that she never seemed satisfied in Missouri anymore. She longed for Kansas.

Chapter 45

Life went on as usual for me. I was so happy to be back with my good friends and to the free and easy life again.

One of our special times was cider time. The ladies washed the apples and cut them up to see that no worms were put into the press. I didn't see them make it, but they brought gallon stone jugs of it home, and it was so good.

The ladies made dozens of fresh doughnuts. It was another time for the people to get together at the big hall to visit, drink the fresh cider, and eat the doughnuts.

It was a little noisy with all the children playing around. We played outside as long as we could see, playing hide-and-go-seek. One night I fell into a barbed-wire fence and a barb stuck into my eyebrow so deep that I still have the scar.

Aunt Meg Fort wasn't really our aunt. She had lived in Quick City for a long time.

She was one of the McCoy girls. (I don't know if the Hatfields lived around there or not.) They came from the south someplace to Missouri.

She married a Mr. George. They had Lily Mae, Clifford, Florence, and Laura. When they were quite young, Mr. George died.

Later she married a Mr. Fort, who had Preston, Ellen, and Jessie. They were all grown up and all married except Clifford, Florence, and Preston.

Lily Mae married Daddy's cousin Robert Moore, my cousin Clyde's parents. They later had two more sons, Scott and Robert.

Jessie Fort Reed was the lady I was named for. I got to see her in 1948 when I visited Aunt Cora Belle. She gave me a pretty scarf and took me out to lunch.

Preston, or Press, as we called him lived in Kansas City. He came to visit and always brought us presents. He told me I was his girl, and he would come back and marry me when I grew up. I was eight or nine at the time and he was about twenty-five. Mama said Press spoiled us more than we already were. We always thought of these people as our relatives.

Mama's sister Janette came to visit us and stayed on, as Mama had done. Clifford George came home from Warrensburg College and met Aunt Janette. He spent a lot of time at our home. It wasn't long until he married our auntie, and they lived close by.

A new store building had been built. It was much larger than the old one. It had a nice little post office built on one side. Everyone had a box that was built into the wall. The boxes were numbered, and the families knew their number.

Uncle Clifford was now the postmaster and the grocery man. There were some nice rooms in the back where he and Aunt Janette lived.

The store part was a huge room with everything piled in it. There were long counters and shelves filled full of merchandise. There was material to make clothes, ribbons, lace, buttons, pins, needles; it was almost like going to Holden.

There were also shelves for groceries, sacks of flour and sugar, barrels of apples, crates of oranges, but there was no lettuce or fresh meat. Everyone had their own meat, butchered as needed.

There were big round boxes of cheese on the counter, and a glass case with the candy in it to keep the flies off and the children out, I imagine. On the counters were also large boxes of crackers and gingersnaps. They kept lard in large tin cans, and some salt pork, meat that had been cured well, also.

Next was the tobacco shelf, with Sir Walter Raleigh for the pipes, plug chewing tobacco, and boxes of snuff.

When the train came with the mail, the man threw the sack of mail onto the platform at the depot and took the one that was waiting for him. Someone would grab the mail sack and take it to the store.

Uncle Clifford would open it. Usually there was a line of people or children waiting. He would call out the names and if no one answered, he put it into a box on the wall. If the mail was given to the children, we were told to go straight home with that mail *now*. Getting letters was a great event in our lives.

Chapter 46

One day Mama was getting ready to make a Christmas plum pudding. This had to be made some time before it was ready to eat; the pudding was soaked in brandy.

She sent me to the store to get some cinnamon, nutmeg, and suet and not forget what I went after.

"Oh, I won't forget," I said, and off I went.

On the way I met Clyde. We stopped to visit awhile, then I hurried to the store and told Uncle Clifford I wanted some Susan.

He asked, "Are you sure that's what Maggie wants?"

I said yes.

He asked what kind of a box did it come in.

I didn't know.

At last he asked what she was doing or making.

I told him she was making a plum pudding and he said well, he thought she wanted some suet.

He gave me a large chunk and asked what else.

I had forgotten the other things. I finally remembered cinnamon and nutmeg and rushed home.

Mama said, "Well, you took long enough. Did Uncle Clifford have to butcher a cow to get it?"

I skipped away fast. I didn't want her to know that I had forgotten what I was sent for.

Uncle Clifford told her anyway, and she said, "When will that child get her head out of the clouds and pay attention to what she is told?"

Mama was glad to have Aunt Janette there, and they spent as much time together as they could. Mama had so much work at home, and Aunt Janette helped in the store.

My brother, Lynn, got into trouble one day. He had watched Mama go to the store, get the things she wanted, get a little piece of paper, put it in her purse, and take the things and go home. He was very fond of cheese and decided he could get his cheese this way.

He started going to the store and buying a dime's worth of cheese. Uncle Clifford didn't doubt that Mama had sent Lynn for the cheese, so he gave it to him with the ticket, which he either lost or tore up.

After he did this several times through the month, Uncle Clifford wondered what Mama was doing with so much cheese.

Mama always figured the store bill, and on pay-up night, Daddy took the bills and went to the store to pay our grocery bill. Uncle Clifford would take our tickets, mark them "paid," and give them back to Daddy with his tickets, too.

This time they didn't match the ones Daddy had.

He took the tickets to Mama and said, "I

guess you made a little mistake this time."

Mama looked at Uncle Clifford's tickets and found all that cheese she hadn't bought. The next day she went to the store and asked Uncle Clifford which one of us had come for the cheese.

She was very surprised to learn that it was her little son. Uncle Clifford told her he wouldn't let him have any more unless he brought a note from her. She said that he wouldn't ask for any more.

She came home, called Lynn, and told him how wrong it was for him to go to the store when she didn't send him. Then she switched him, to help him remember.

She didn't switch him as hard as she would have Tressie or me, because he was the baby of the family and had a crippled foot. She never could punish him very much.

I used to think it would be nice to be the youngest of the family. I was always told that I must do this or that because I was the oldest of the children.

I have always been thankful that my mother was wise enough to switch my legs with those little willow branches. They did no permanent damage, and a lot of good.

I'm also glad that when she promised anything she always kept her word. She was wonderful and loved us very much.

Chapter 47

Daddy had an aunt Janette Elliott who lived on a beautiful farm near Latour, Missouri. She and Uncle Ruben would invite Tressie and me to visit them after school was out.

What a thrill that was! Their son John would come for us with the horse and buggy and drive us to the farm. Good thing there were no automobiles to pass on those roads; they were so narrow and winding, it would have been trouble. It was paradise for us, their house was so large and the yard so nice.

John was a student at Warrensburg College and would tell us stories of his life there. They were mostly made up for our entertainment, I'm sure. He teased us a lot, too.

They had a nice hammock made of wire and barrel staves. It was tied between two large trees. Aunt Nettie put a little mattress that she had made on it. We liked to lie in it. John would come up quietly and pretend to dump us out, just to hear us scream. Aunt Nettie would yell, "John, stop teasing my girls!" We thought John knew most everything.

His brother Robert had married a girl named Edna Anderson; they had a baby girl, Ruby, who still lives near the old farm. We used to walk to their house to play with little Ruby. She is the only one of that family still living, and is a lovely person. I have visited her three times since 1946. I have only a few cousins still living in Missouri.

Aunt Nettie had lovely houseplants in a room with windows on all sides, and a lemon tree that grew in a large tub painted green. It had pretty lemons on it.

Aunt Nettie would take us to Latour with her to shop. We took the surrey pulled by two horses. It was a spring-type wagon, only much nicer. It had a top over it with a fringe around it. Sure was fun riding in it. We would come home with new hair ribbons and material for new dresses for Mama to sew for us, and I always got some more pretty beads.

How we hated to see the day come when we had to go home. It was usually a Sunday when Uncle Rube and Aunt Nettie would take us in the surrey and spend the day with our parents.

Aunt Nettie had a wonderful voice and was asked to sing at weddings and funerals or church gatherings. Uncle Clifford, who sang with her lots of times, said that she was the only woman he had ever heard of who could sing any part, tenor, alto, soprano, or bass. Uncle Clifford sang tenor.

One time he had a music teacher come from Kansas City to give him lessons. The teacher heard me singing and wanted to give me lessons, too. Mama said we couldn't afford it. The teacher said, "Too bad, too bad."

I had a lot of fun singing, even if I didn't know how. We all loved the old hymns and sang a lot at home. Mama wasn't much of a singer, but Daddy, Tressie, and I made a lot of noise.

Lynn played more by himself, playing with his toys and Dandy. He didn't make friends easy like I did. Tressie and her friends fought one day and made up the next. She got angry real easy. Her temper would scare a bear away.

We had more cousins in the country; Mike and Nettie Brooks were Mama's relatives. Their children were Inez, who went to Warrensburg College, Iola, Hazel, Cecil, Birdie Lee (my age), and two boys, Eugene and Norman.

I remember one cold Thanksgiving we were invited to their home for dinner. We went in a big farm wagon with Uncle Frank and Aunt Dora Lee and their family. The ladies put chairs in the back of the wagon and wrapped up in blankets. All of us children were piled on the floor.

Hay had been put in, then covered with blankets put on top, so with our heavy clothing and more blankets plus hot rocks placed in the wagon, we were nice and warm. Those rocks had been placed in the oven overnight, then wrapped good so they wouldn't get that hot. Only five miles, but it took a long time to drive through the snow.

Short distances we went on bobsleds, with bells on the horses' bridles or harnesses jingling all the way. Sometimes they tipped us out in the snow. Fun anyway —

When we got to the Brookses' we were relieved to get out of the cramped conditions we were in. We were so hungry, too.

It was the custom for the grown-ups to eat first while the children played. Who could play when you were starving.

At last we were called to the table, and there was so much food. Cousin Nettie must have cooked for days.

We got home real late; must have been ten o'clock.

It was a Thanksgiving to remember, a

house full of cousins, all talking at once. It was our last one in Missouri. Mama's health, never good, became worse, and she wanted to move back to Kansas.

In the spring of 1910 we decided to make the move back to Kansas to please Mama. I had my eleventh birthday and thought I was nearly a grown-up. I sure didn't want to leave Missouri.

Mama insisted we should be raised up around her people. I guess she didn't realize how hard it would be to transplant a Missourian.

It hadn't been so bad just thinking we would move someday, but the closer the time came to really leave, the more Tressie, Lynn, and I hated it.

Aunt Mel Higgins promised to take care of Dandy until we were settled, then they would send him to us. That dog was precious to us. (It was a good thing we didn't know when we left that we would never see our dog or those dear people again. When I did go back in 1946 they were all dead or had moved away.)

Anyway, Aunt Mel wrote that Dandy had grieved himself to death — wouldn't eat or leave the yard where we had lived. One day they found him dead. She said they buried him in her backyard.

That was our last train ride for years, and the trip was not very interesting. Daddy kept telling us not to worry, we would go back to visit. It just didn't happen.

So ended my life in Missouri — no more fishing anytime I wanted to, and I was leaving all my good friends and family. I didn't see Aunt Cora Belle or Aunt Dora Lee for years.

Daddy and us kids were to become misplaced persons.

PART II

WORLD WAR I

(1910-1919)

Chapter 48

We arrived here in Manhattan tired and unhappy; all except Mama. She was coming home at last.

What a different life we had come to. Right from the first we began to realize we were a little different from our Kansas relatives.

We stayed a few days with Grandma and Grandpa until we found a little house close by. Daddy got work of some kind, I don't remember what.

First, we moved a block away, to Seventh Street. Grandpa and Grandma owned their house on Sixth Street. These houses were across both railroad tracks. Grandma had pretty flowers and a nice garden. I always liked to visit her; she was good to us.

We had been taught that anyone who behaved properly and obeyed the laws of the land and went to church were all right people, one as good as the other. It made no difference what they wore or how they made their living, as long as they were honest. If a man wasn't sick, he was supposed to work and take care of his family. If you were sick, the neighbors and relatives came and cared for you and your family until you were able to work again. You returned the favor when someone else needed help. There was no pay; it would have been an insult to offer money to anyone offering their help. If you had more fruit or vegetables than you needed, you gave it to whoever didn't have enough.

Here it was a different story. Our furnishings had been shipped on the train, and it was a job getting unpacked and things arranged in that house. It was smaller than we were used to and not as nice, either. No one offered to come and help. Only Aunt Louise, the one of Mama's sisters who had several children and lived on a farm. She took Tressie and Lynn to her home for a few days and sent in some fresh vegetables.

I guess the other sisters didn't want to get dirty. Anyway, they didn't come near. No one paid any attention to us at all except one family across the alley from us, the Campbells, who became lifelong friends. They had three children: Jesse, Etta, and Wesley.

Mama said after we had lived there a while it would be different. Her folks were so different from Daddy's, I never felt at ease around them. I knew they were comparing me to their children and finding me batting zero.

I had never felt self-conscious before, but now I did. Mama's sisters objected to our way of talking, and I heard her oldest sister, Rose, tell her sister Daisy that we were backwoods hillbillies. They referred to my dad as a "country hick."

She referred to our way of talking as ridiculous, and I imagine it did sound strange to them. If we were asked where something was, we would say, "Over yonder," or "On yon side of the road a piece," or ask someone to "come and set a spell with us." We would say, "You all stay with us," when someone started to leave. I expect our lingo did hurt their ears.

Only Aunt Rose acted like we had crawled out from under a rock. She was ashamed of us. Her children did all the right things.

I asked Mama what a hillbilly was or a country hick.

She said, "Never you mind. I am going to have a talk with your aunt Rosie."

After that she said we would stay on our side of the fence. Only thing was we didn't have a fence.

We went to Grandma's often. She was so

nice and talked softly and made us feel welcome.

It was great to have a grandma and grandpa. I was always a little in awe of Grandpa. He didn't have so much to say to us and was always busy. Grandma knew what we liked to eat and she cooked fried cabbage in bacon grease, and sour cream or vinegar. It was so good. So was our cornbread. She also made fried potatoes and onions. She asked us to eat with her often.

I was eleven years old, and my youngest aunt was sixteen. I liked her a lot. Of course she wasn't home much.

I liked Uncle Jesse, too. He was a large man with brown eyes and red curly hair. He was always good to me; he said it was because I was his namesake.

At the end of the street where we lived was a large white house with a greenhouse. (It is still there.) It was owned by the Moore family at that time. They lived in the house and sold flowers and plants from their greenhouse. They delivered flowers with a horse and wagon.

They had two children, Floyd and Thelma. In the evenings they, the Campbell children, and Tressie, Lynn, and I gathered to play until dark. Slowly I began to like Manhattan.

The trains going by reminded me of home. These train men would always wave to us as they went by.

Chapter 49

Mama started to try to change our way of talking. She talked right, like all her folks, and by fall when school started, we were doing much better.

While we lived on Sixth Street, Lynn, Tressie, and I had the measles. Mama heard that many children had them and expected we would, too.

She asked Grandma who their doctor was these days. Grandma said that Dr. William Clarkson, a nice young man, seemed to be a good doctor. When Tressie got sick, Mama called him.

He came and said that yes, Tressie had the measles and he expected that Lynn and I would get them, too.

Tressie soon felt well again. Lynn took them, but had a light case.

Then I got very ill, with a high fever, but the measles wouldn't break out on me. Dr. Clarkson came and wrapped me in blankets with hot-water bottles. I was freezing, or thought I was. He made me drink some whiskey and ginger or nutmeg, or some kind of spice, in hot water. It tasted terrible.

He said those measles had to break out and that fever had to go down fast. Strange how you can have a fever and feel so cold. He stayed until I fell asleep.

That night we had a bad storm; a tornado had struck in Omaha, Nebraska, nearly destroying it. Mama was worried; she had sick children and no storm cellar.

The next morning was nice again and I was all red with measles.

We still missed our friends in Missouri and dreamed of going back. We missed them dropping by to set a spell.

When school was about ready to start Aunt Rosie told Mama that Tressie and I would surely be put back a grade or two, below her daughter, who was my age.

When Mama asked why, Aunt Rosie said, "Well, because they went to that old country school. Ours are so much more advanced."

Mama said, "You may have better buildings, I agree there. But our schoolteachers were good ones. They were trained at Warrensburg College and knew how to teach just as well as the ones here do."

Mama came home, called us inside, and said, "Listen here," and she told us what Auntie had said. Then she said, "We will show her a thing or two. I want you to take your report cards and go to your proper grade, and do your very best to stay there."

And we did. We were admitted to our classrooms and remained there. To have failed would have been a disgrace and broken Mama's heart.

Daddy didn't say anything. He knew he and his children were outsiders. For Mama's sake he always kept quiet, going to work each day, steady and strong. He was our rock to cling to. He made new friends and joined the Odd Fellows Lodge.

I wasn't the best student in the class by far, but I managed to get by. I liked history, reading, spelling, and English, even if I did mangle it up a lot in talking. I still do.

Arithmetic I hated. I thought I knew enough. I could add, subtract, and count any money I would ever have, so why worry? I was right about that; my money was never enough to need much counting. (Kenny, that calculator you gave me does it all for me, thanks again.) I knew enough for what I was destined to do.

After Aunt Rosie saw that we weren't going to disgrace her and her little brood she became more friendly, and as the years passed we often visited in her home. She wasn't so bad once we got used to her.

Chapter 50

I never felt close to Mama's relatives, or most of them, anyway. Aunt Louise and Uncle John Hunter were exceptions. They were some of the finest people I have ever known. It was always a joy to go to their home.

They lived on Hunter's Island on a nice farm. They had six children. Florence and Lois were the same ages as Tressie and me. In those first years we were here in Manhattan, I don't know as we would have managed without them.

Uncle John played the violin, and some of his friends played guitars. Sometimes they would take all the furniture out of the living room and all the neighbors would come and they had a dance. The children would come too. I loved that music. There was so much talking, eating, and everyone was happy.

There were box suppers at the schoolhouse, and many programs. I was always invited to go with Florence.

One day I walked from our home to theirs. It was Easter time. I had just crossed the bridge that Saturday morning and got to Aunt Louise's house when a man named Costello tried to cross with some kind of heavy equipment. The bridge broke in two and he and the machinery fell into the water. He was mashed to death. He had been warned not to try to cross; the bridge had a sign posted saying loads of a certain weight should not cross. I had to stay at Aunt Louise's home until they fixed a way for us to walk over again.

Those first years in Manhattan there were no paved streets, except for Poyntz Avenue, and not too many sidewalks. They were putting new sidewalks in all the time. There weren't many houses, either. There were streetcars running on tracks, weaving through the street on the north side of Poyntz Avenue and to Aggieville. It cost a nickel to ride.

We attended the old Central School, now called Woodrow Wilson. It was so different from what we were used to. It was a beautiful old stone building with ivy growing over it. It had many rooms with rest rooms in the basement. It sure wasn't like our one-room school with the old outhouses. This was really nice. My first teacher was Miss Minnie Diebler, I loved her. She laughed at me, too, but in a friendly way.

My grandmother did a lot of tatting, or lacework. She made what they called jabots. The ladies wore them where their dress collars fastened at the neck in front. They had pretty velvet ribbon on them.

Miss Diebler wanted some very much. Grandma made her two, and I took them to school for her. She sent back two dollars to pay for them. I decided to learn to tat and make myself a lot of money. Ha, ha —

My next teacher was Miss Ivy Green. She was nice, too.

I made new friends at school; Frances Harrop was my favorite girl. My mother had known her folks years before. I thought she was the prettiest girl I had ever seen. I wanted to be like her. I liked her mother a lot, too.

When we were twelve years old, our mothers let us have what they called corselettes, and we thought we were all grown up. I sure didn't need it, I was still so skinny. I just did whatever Frances did.

I liked Harriet and Louise Moffett, too. They were the daughters of Dr. Moffett, who was a prominent doctor in Manhattan for many years.

Joe Burr, Scott Rhutze, Harry and Everett Wareham, and Burdette Tegehier, who was a pretty little girl with golden curls. There were too many to name here. They were nice youngsters, and school was fun.

Only when the boys teased me for being so skinny was I unhappy at school. On windy days they would yell, "Hello, Skinny Jessie! Hope you put rocks in your pockets so you won't blow away!" I got so angry —

It wasn't because I didn't eat enough. Mama used to say, "Child, where do you put all that food? I guess it makes you skinny to carry it around."

Chapter 51

We moved from Sixth Street to 1114 Yuma. It was another nice neighborhood. I liked it better; the house was much nicer. We had water in the house and electric lights.

It was farther to school, but that didn't matter. There were several children to walk with. Sarah and John Anglin lived on the southeast corner of the block. We were near the middle of the block on the north side of the street. There was a family named

Coffman, one named Sphinks, and the Tyson family lived on the northeast corner.

Eva Tyson was a grade ahead of me, but we walked to school together most mornings. She was a very sweet girl. I liked her mother; she was friendly and always nice to us.

Across the alley was John Anderson, with his wife, Stella, and daughter, Mabel. She was older than I. She was allowed to have a boyfriend. I used to carry notes for her and her friend. His name was Winfield Walker. He moved away from here many years ago. His brother Bill worked for Rexall Drugstore for a long time. Their mother, Josephine, became a very good friend of mine in later years.

It seemed that I soon knew half the town.

Mama didn't go many places, to church when she was able and to the Rebekah Lodge. We bought groceries at the little store in the 600 block of Colorado Street. Dick Short and his family owned it.

Mama ordered what she wanted and Arthur Scheleen was the delivery boy. He worked some hours in a shoe store downtown in his spare time. We went past his home to go to school, and he would walk along with us to Poyntz Ave. He used to tell me I was his girlfriend. I thought he was

154

the nicest young man in town.

I remember when they started the new school on Poyntz Avenue. It had been the old Avenue School, now it was the new junior high school. (Your grandfathers both worked on that building, doing the cement work. Your father's dad, Grandpa Henry, and two other men were contractors who had their own company and did most of the cement work and bricklaying around town. Grandpa was extra good at building chimneys and fireplaces. He did a lot of work at the college. My dad worked with them. I used to stop and watch them work on my way home from school.)

I started school there the year it was finished. They didn't have the kitchen finished, so our home economics class would walk to the college on the afternoons set aside for that class, and there we started learning to cook. That's where I learned to fix the baked cabbage and cheese you all like so much.

The years slipped by, and life was good in Manhattan. There were no orchards or large gardens, and no place near to go fishing, and I sure missed that, but we had many conveniences we hadn't had before. We had a bathroom and a gas stove to cook on, electric lights, a better washing machine, and for the first time we had life insurance. A man came each month to collect the money for it.

We never had money for any extras. I asked Daddy why we didn't ever have any money anymore, and he said it cost so much more to live in Manhattan, and Mama had to have money for her doctor bills and medicine. Then he said, "Money isn't everything, honey. Most ways we are very well off. We can all see, hear, and walk. The whole world is ours to enjoy — the flowers, birds, beautiful buildings, and the parks. They are all as much ours as anyone's to look at and admire. We all have good health except Mama, and we can keep these things because the memory of them will stay in our hearts and minds forever." (How right he was.)

Chapter 52

I walked to First Baptist Church each Sunday. It was at Seventh and Humboldt, a beautiful building. We had our Sunday school class in the balcony. Miss Reba Wolk was our teacher. I'll never forget the nice parties she had for us at her home on Fifth and Humboldt. We had parties for Washington's birthday, Halloween, Valentine's Day. We all loved her and her sister Nell.

When I was fourteen years old, I had my first boyfriend, Walter Stacy. He was messenger boy for the telegraph company. He worked on Saturdays and after school. He wore a uniform and cap and rode a bicycle.

He started coming to our home. Mama and Daddy liked him. After a few evenings spent at home, they decided we might be allowed to go to the movies and some parties.

One night we forgot the time. (I always had a curfew.) This time I was nearly an hour late.

My punishment was to stay home for a week. No shows. I could go only to school and church.

Mama had another sick spell, and Reverend Jacobson, our new minister, came to call. I had met him, but the rest of the family hadn't.

He came to call on Mama, and Tressie met him at the porch and said, "If you have come to take Jessie Lee someplace, you might as well go back."

He asked why, and Tressie said, "Because

she didn't come home on time and has to stay home."

He laughed and said he wanted to see Mama. He came in and told me I had better mind my mother after this.

I said, "Yes, sir," and quickly left the room.

He often came to visit us and have prayers with Mama while she was sick, and he always teased me about being home on time.

Some of the church members who lived on farms would let our Sunday school classes come there to have nice picnics. We were taken on big hay wagons, or racks, and enjoyed those days so much. We sang songs going and coming. It's a wonder the horses didn't get scared and run away, we made so much noise.

Our church was always a nice place to go. Most of the people I knew then are gone now. I can still see them as they were then. Strange how we remember people as they were in past years and how different they seem when we meet them again in later years.

I wonder how many people here remember the old fountain in the park and those large, fat goldfish, so pretty swimming around there. That park was always full of children. It was a fine place to play.

Reverend Jacobson baptized me in 1913. He left Manhattan many years ago and is quite old now. I always think of him as a wonderful young man who was kind to us all.

Chapter 53

Mama wouldn't allow me to learn to dance. All the young boys and girls were learning. I thought I was the only one in town who couldn't go dancing. That's how I lost my Walter; he learned to dance. Oh, well, I found out there were others who had mothers that believed the same way mine did. As I had never been to the hall, I didn't know what I was missing.

Daddy used to take me to town with him on Saturday nights and let me go to the movie. He would go to the Odd Fellows Hall. I would wait for him and we would walk home together.

One night I asked him if it was true that the devil ran the dances.

He said he reckoned the devil was around most every place. He didn't see any harm in dancing, as long as you behaved yourself, like a lady should.

I wanted to go see how it was done. So the next Saturday, instead of the movie, he took me to the Woodman's Hall (that was in the old Marshall building), where the dances were held.

It was mostly a family gathering. I knew many of the people there. Daddy asked some of his friends to keep an eye on me and said he would be back to take me home.

I loved that music, and people swinging around the floor. Soon some of the kids wanted to teach me how it was done. I felt like everyone was watching me. I think a guilty conscience kept me from being very good at it.

After that night, that's where I spent most of my Saturday nights. Daddy always came to take me home. Mama didn't find out for a long time.

Chapter 54

In our first years in Manhattan, Aunt Rose lived in the north part of town, between Kearney and Vattier on Fourth Street. Sometimes she seemed to forget we were hillbillies and asked us to stay a few days with Olive. She could be real nice. We got to know all her neighbors, like the Rodgers family. Mr. Rodgers was a policeman, Ada and Flossie were his girls, and Orville and Trueman were his boys. They were all older than me except Flossie; she was my age.

The Faley family lived on Kearney Street in the big house at 323. My grandparents had lived there when my mother was a little girl. It was called the pink house then. It had been painted a bright pink and was the only house in the block. There was a large barn at the east end of the block, where the tire shop is now, on Third Street. It was there until sometime in the 1930s. It was then made into a house. Grandpa kept his horses there. The rest of the land was used as a garden and yard.

I have been told by my mother that some people are buried in that yard someplace, and some babies in the old cellar under the house. They had died of diphtheria. It seemed there was an epidemic of it in Manhattan one time and many people died of it. Mama said whenever she was sent to the cellar for vegetables, she would hurry as fast as she could to get out of there. I guess someone had told her some ghost stories, too.

Mama told me how the old Blue River had flowed along where Tuttle Creek Boulevard now is and how the flood of 1908 had changed its course and left only a small stream, which grew smaller as time passed.

Another neighbor was the William Clapp family. They had one son, Alfred. They lived at 315 Thurston for many years. They had lots of flowers, and cookies for all children who came there.

On the corner of Fourth and Thurston lived the Ikenhorst family. Their children were Mary, Lottie, Emma, and Bertha. They were my friends as long as they lived. The mother and father sold milk and eggs, and I remember how neat and clean their place always was. They used the land around them for pasture; there were no houses in that block. So the chickens and cows had plenty of room. I used to go there with my cousin Olive to buy milk and eggs.

Across the street, where Goodnow Park is now, was all pastureland. The Niemiers kept their cattle there. They lived on the east side of Fourth Street.

We think the snow is bad now, but that old mud was worse. Horses had a time pulling delivery wagons through the streets, and most people ordered their groceries by phone. That mud would be so deep, and as it dried, the streets were all rough ridges. There were brick sidewalks as far as Kearney Street.

I spent a lot of time at the Faley home. Arlene, Fremont, and Gladys are the ones I remember. Arlene became a schoolteacher in the Manhattan schools. I sometimes stayed overnight with Gladys. The Niemier family were Emma, Helen, and Norman. I knew them all well, and we were always good friends.

Chapter 55

Time passed so quickly, there was so much to do and so many places to go.

A favorite place of mine was the old library on Fifth Street between Poyntz and Humboldt. It was a meeting place for the young kids after school, Saturdays, or whenever they could manage to get there.

I have sat there on those steps talking for hours and have read a lot of books from the inside.

Mama often sent me to get books for her. She would make a list of the authors she liked best. The librarian would find them for me.

I don't suppose there were many feet of ground on Bluemont Hill or Old Prospect I haven't walked over. That was a Sunday afternoon pastime. Several of us would start walking, and first thing we knew we were climbing one of the hills (our mountains).

The first time I climbed old Bluemont, I thought I would never reach the top. It was a fight all the way. I had to catch hold of bushes that grew all over to keep from falling. Many children have had broken bones from falling down that hill. It was almost straight up, and we were glad to rest once we reached the top.

Up there was a great cement tank filled with water. It was the city reservoir. It was enclosed with heavy wire netting to protect one from falling in. It was worth the climb, you could see so far in all directions.

We all liked playing at the City Park or going to the college and sliding down an old fire escape on one of the buildings. It was round and we would climb to the top, get in, and have a fast trip to the bottom, where we slid out. Then we'd climb up the ladder to do it over again, one after the other. It was great fun. No one ever told us not to. It was taken to City Park many years later for children to play on there.

There were the Memorial Day parades that started at the East River Bridge, where flowers were thrown in the water in honor of navy dead, and then marched up Poyntz Avenue to the cemetery. I used to march along with them. Large crowds of people would be gathered there, putting flowers on graves. Some men would talk about the dead soldiers who had given their lives for us so we might be free. Little flags were put on their graves. We would wander around, looking at names on headstones and the beautiful flowers.

Later came commencement exercises at the college. The graduates paraded around in their caps and long black gowns, looking so grown-up and important. They had prominent men there to speak to them, and they were handed their diplomas. It was so exciting to me, I decided I wanted to go to college, too, but fate decided otherwise.

The Fourth of July, Independence Day, came with flags flying, firecrackers popping, and celebrations in City Park. There were more speeches and always a young man reciting the Declaration of Independence. It made us feel proud to be Americans.

I suppose we had dishonest politicians then, too. The old saying "What you don't know won't hurt you" is all wrong, I think. People of today are having the troubles we have because we didn't know or care enough to do anything about it back then. We closed our eyes to the wrongdoing of men in high places, and just see where it has led.

America is still the most wonderful place on earth, but it sure needs a lot of house-cleaning in high places. When people stop treating these men and women who fight so hard for an office like gods instead of paid employees, we will get someplace. All men created equal? Ha! Then why is there so much hero worship for men who steal the country blind? It is the people who need to wake up and fly right, get a few morals, and some honesty before it is too late. (Sorry, didn't mean to preach, but you all know me. So much for independence and free speech.)

There was an amusement park at a big lake out where the Odd Fellows Home has been for so many years. The lake was very nice. People went there to swim and could hire rowboats for twenty-five cents an hour.

One Fourth of July, they were having a big celebration, like you sometimes read about but seldom ever see. I wanted to go very much, but I knew Mama couldn't take me. She never went where there were large crowds.

One of Mama's friends, Sarah Anglin, said, "Maggie, Jessie Lee can go with us." So I got to go.

The streetcar, or Interurban car, came right by our house, and I was up and ready long before time to leave. Mama gave me some money, told me to behave myself and not to be a bother to Sarah.

I promised and ran to the corner to join the other neighbors waiting for the streetcar. Soon we were there.

Such a crowd was gathered in the park that day. There were great food stands with all kinds of goodies: pink lemonade, candied popcorn, and sandwiches, a great diet for the young. On the lake people were rowing around, singing. There were bands playing, firecrackers popping, and the speeches. We walked miles, all over that park. It was a wonderful day.

It was getting near time to go home when I met Frank Davis. He was my Aunt Florence's brother-in-law and my good friend. He was alone, with his horse and buggy, and he asked me to go back with him.

I was delighted, so I hurried to find Sarah to tell her. Instead I found her daughter

Beatrice and told her to tell her mama I was going home with Frank. She said, "Fine, go on."

Well, the Interurban traveled much faster than Frank's horse, and it was late when we got home.

Mama was waiting for me and she was very upset. She really blessed me out; scared poor Frank speechless. Then she recognized Frank and told him she was sorry, she wouldn't have worried if she had known I was with him.

I learned not to go someplace one way and come home another. Even Daddy was cross with me. Mama had seen the people get off the car, and when I wasn't there she started imagining all sorts of things. (Just like I have done so many times when some of mine have been late.)

She talked to Sarah, and Sarah said not to worry, I would be all right. I had told Beatrice I was coming home with a friend, but they couldn't remember his name. Sarah always stayed calm; Mama didn't.

Chapter 56

My first job was at the Duckwall Store — the five-and-ten-cent store, it was called. It really had a lot of things for that price.

Mr. Leslie Wagaman was the manager. He was a friend of my father's.

I asked him for a job for summer vacation. He thought I was too young, but said I could try it, and I liked it very much.

I liked waiting on the customers who came into the store, except for one lady. She kept roomers or college students. She came to me and said, "Miss, I want to buy two dozen cups." She didn't want the saucers and said she should have the cups cheaper without them.

I told her that I couldn't sell one without the other.

She got as mad as a hornet that's had its nest destroyed. She said, "I will report you to the manager and you will lose your job. I have all the saucers I want. I need those cups."

We had been told never to sell one without the other, so I still refused.

Again she said she was going to get me fired and that I was an impudent girl.

I told her to go ahead, and see if I cared. I did care, but I wasn't going to let her know it.

Then Mr. Wagaman came along and asked what was going on.

She replied, "This girl has been arguing with me. I want to buy two dozen cups and she won't sell them to me."

He looked at me and asked why.

I replied, "You said not to sell the cup without the saucer, or the saucer without the cup, didn't you?"

He said, "You bet I did, and I won't, either." He turned to the lady and said, "Sorry, madam, but she was only doing as instructed. I don't believe anyone else will sell them that way, either."

She turned and flounced out of the store so fast, it was a wonder she didn't fall and break a leg.

After she left he gave me a pat on the shoulder and said, "Good girl, Jessie Lee."

Most of the people who came into the store were nice. I worked until school started. Mr. Wagaman gave me a recommendation that I still have. It reads: "I have employed Miss Brown and found her to be an honest and capable saleslady."

The next summer Duckwall's had enough help, so I went to Woolworth's. They had just started a store here, and I worked there until school started in the fall.

Chapter 57

We moved from 1114 Yuma to a house across the street from Grandma, on Sixth Street. Our neighbors were Will and Ella Reed. Their children were Eunice, Mildred, Elizabeth, Harrison, Wilber, and Leslie.

Fred and Violet Anderson were neighbors, too. I don't recall the children's names, only a daughter, Alene. Fred took tickets at the Wareham Theater. He seemed to like us all and often gave us tickets to the movies. Charlie Chaplin was a favorite, and it cost a nickel for children to go. Nickels were precious in those days.

The very first movie I ever saw in Manhattan or anyplace else was at the old Wareham Theater that was then on the west side of the 400 block of Poyntz. The screen was small and the pictures were blue in color and silent. A man stood at one side of the screen and told the story of the pictures.

There was not a sound from anyone. This was called the matinee. We sat on our seats spellbound, watching those comedies, all that for one nickel. I just wish you all could see some of those early films. You would know how very much movies have changed in my lifetime.

Grandpa Pauley took sick with kidney trouble of some kind. As time went by, he lost his memory and thought he saw little men running around. He insisted they were taking the grapes. We kids thought it was funny, but today I know it was a tragedy and was very real to him.

He soon died, and Grandma was so tired from taking care of him (she had insisted on doing everything herself). They had been very happy, and after he died she just didn't seem to care about anything. She would sit in her old rocking chair, paying no attention to anyone. She answered questions, and cared for herself, but refused to leave the place. I guess she was reliving old memories.

In a short time, she was gone too. Dr. Clarkson said she just didn't want to live without Grandpa. It must be wonderful for a husband and wife to care that much.

I will never forget my gentle, loving grandma, and how she taught me tatting.

She had come to our house one day and said she had come to teach me to tat. I had watched her doing it so often and told her I wanted to learn. She handed me the shuttle and showed me how to hold the thread.

I tried and tried, with no luck. I was the type of child that, if something seemed too hard, would lose interest and try something else. But the family all knew that if they made me angry, I would manage somehow to learn whatever it was I was trying to do.

Now I laid that shuttle aside and told her, "I can't do that," and started to leave the room.

She said, "Oh, well, I didn't think you could. I will teach Tressie."

Well, that did it. I grabbed that shuttle, and under the table I went, and there I stayed until I could make that stitch. It wasn't long until I was making lace.

She laughed about it later. She said, "I knew you could do it if you would try hard enough."

As you all know, I have never stopped tatting. That little shuttle has been my pacifier through the years. The more disturbed I have been, the faster I have tatted.

Chapter 58

I finished the tenth grade and then I had to stop school and stay home to take over Mama's work. She had become very ill. I had everything to do: bake bread, the washing, keep the house, try to cook, and take care of Mama.

Dr. Clarkson called Dr. Colt Sr. to come and see if he could decide what was wrong. They didn't do tests like they do these days.

One thing she did have was anemia. They gave her a tonic of beef liver and wine, a favorite tonic of the time for anemia patients.

As I was the nurse, I had a lot to remember. Dr. Clarkson made me a chart with the time for each medicine marked on it.

Mama was in bed several weeks. It took a long time for her to get strength enough to walk around, and I was tired out.

Daddy helped all he could. Tressie, being younger, didn't have to do much she didn't want to.

Where, oh, where were Mama's sisters all those long dreary days? They came by for

Jessie Lee in ROTC garb, Lucas, Kansas, age 16.

little visits sometimes, or sent her some little thing they had fixed for her to eat. Mostly, we managed without their help.

Mama had an uncle who lived in Lucas, Kansas. He was a doctor, the only one there at the time. He wrote to Mama, telling her that if we would come there, he would like to look after her, and he thought the air would do her good. He said a change in climate often helped people.

Mama and Daddy talked it over, and Daddy made a trip to see if he could find work and a place to live. He did, so off we went again. We lived there for the next two years.

How I hated it those first few weeks! I missed the trees and Manhattan, where my friends were. It was a small place. All I wanted was to get back to Manhattan.

We had a nice home, and Tressie, Lynn, and I started going to the Baptist church. Mama had a cousin living there, Eva Pauley Simmons, with her husband, Ed, and their four children, Loyd, Neil, Edith, and Thelma. Edith was my age, Thelma was Tressie's. They took us around the little town, and soon we had many new friends.

Mama did seem to feel better. She hadn't seen her uncle for many years, so she enjoyed her visits with him and his family. He had two sons, Ray and Riley, a daughter, Mayme, and a granddaughter, Henrietta.

I loved Uncle Doc, and many times when he had to go to the country to see a patient he let me go along. That old horse was slow. He could have had a car — his sons did — but Uncle Doc liked his way best.

I started school in the fall and liked it real well, except when the teacher would say, "Come back and join us, Jessie Lee, you have been dreaming long enough."

Uncle had been a soldier in the War Between the States, and I would ask questions about it. I told him what our friends from Tennessee had said about the way the Yankee soldiers had treated them.

He said, "Yes, it was a very bad time for all."

When I told him I hated the Yankees, he said, "Listen here, my little Rebel, I was there, and I worked with all wounded, both Rebels and Yankees. They were young men doing what they thought right. Some of them were still children. One was no better or worse than the other. It was very bad, that war." He told me how they would run out of supplies and got so hungry it was no wonder they stole all the food they could find.

Uncle Doc's office didn't look much like the ones in Manhattan. He had a big glass showcase where he kept the tools of his trade all locked up, with the medicines he ordered, as needed, from Salina. He allowed me to come to his office, and when he wasn't busy he would tell me what the different instruments were used for and show me how he boiled them in the back room before locking them into the case.

I decided I should become a nurse. I had read all about Florence Nightingale. Uncle Doc discouraged this idea. He said I was far too small for such heavy work. Nurses should be big, strong girls, he said, as they worked in homes many miles from a hospital a good deal of the time. There was no hospital in Lucas. People were taken sixty miles to Salina if they had to have hospital care. So another dream ended, or was put to rest.

There was a little shop across the street from Uncle Doc's office. The lady who owned it hired me to help her on Saturdays and after school. When I wasn't busy I made tatted lace and sold it to the customers when they came in to try on hats or other items.

Chapter 59

My friend Charlie had an old Ford car. Sometimes we would find some friends and drive to Sylvan Grove or Luray, have supper at a café, then drive all around, singing and just enjoying being alive. Instead of the beer of today, we had soda pop — strawberry, cherry, or orange. We liked it.

We had parties in our homes. We played rook and two or three other card games. Not for money, just for the pure joy of winning. (Square? Maybe, but it didn't take much to make us happy.)

Mama got very sick again. A new doctor had come to town and Uncle Doc decided to retire. He was getting very old. I don't remember the new doctor's name, but he was young and the people liked him and his family.

He came to see Mama and said she should be in a hospital.

She said no, so once again I became chief cook, housekeeper, and nurse. This new doctor showed me how to care for my mother and told me how important it was that she got her medicine on time.

Daddy had gone to Manhattan. It was 1916 and we were waiting to move back there to live. I worried that I wouldn't wake up at night to attend to Mama's needs, so I made my bed on the floor beside her bed. We set the alarm to go off at the right time. I would get up, give her the medicine, and set the alarm for the next time.

Daddy came back from Manhattan to help us. It was a very hot summer, and the water supply was low, so we had to be very careful. There was no watering of flowers or gardens.

Mama suffered so much from the heat that the doctor told Daddy to go to the mayor and explain Mama's condition and ask if we might use the hose to sprinkle around the house by her windows. The mayor said yes. We fastened sheets over the windows and kept them soaking wet all day. With the wind blowing through, it worked fine to help keep Mama cool.

Our good friend Sarah Anglin heard of our troubles, and one day she came to take charge. I was never so glad to see anyone in my life. She was like the sunshine after a long cloudy time. When she had to leave, two of Mama's sisters came, Aunt Louise and Aunt Daisy. All together, we brought Mama through a very bad time.

There was one place to go in Lucas that was interesting. It was the Garden of Eden, designed and built by a man named Dinsmore. When I knew him he was an old man with white hair and a beard. Some people said he was off his rocker, but I doubt it. He seemed smart enough to me, and I talked with him many times.

He had gone back to the Bible times of Adam and Eve. He made them of stone and cement. He made the big snake, too. It looked like it might say, "Take the apple, Eve," meaning the one that hung from the branch close by. It was cement, too. Adam and Eve had their fig leaves on. It was really quite wonderful, how he had built it all surrounding his home. He had Old Man Time with his scythe, big birds, and so many, many things.

He had one thing that was spooky. He had built a cement coffin. It was all nicely lined and he insisted he intended to be buried in it. For a dime he would crawl inside and pose as dead for the visitors who came to look at his works of art. Once in there, he laid his arms folded across his chest and closed his eyes. It sure looked real. He enjoyed it and made many dimes that way.

I think it cost twenty-five or fifty cents to tour the garden. I only had to pay the first visit; after that he just let me go there any time I wanted to. I guess he got lonesome, and I liked to talk to him.

He said many times, "They think I am crazy, but I am not."

I asked, "Isn't everyone a little bit crazy, sometimes?"

He said he thought so.

It was fun to wander around there on Sunday afternoons, just to watch the people and hear their remarks. And I liked that old man.

Chapter 60

One time I had a very weird experience in Lucas.

A cousin of my mother's came to visit a sister and brother of hers who lived there. She was a Spiritualist medium, and held what she called séances.

While staying at her brother Arthur's home, she said she couldn't sleep because a spirit kept waking her up. She wanted to have a séance to find out what it wanted.

None of her relatives believed in what they called Inez's foolishness. If I remember right, she finally did have it at Uncle Doc's home. She invited us all to attend.

Mama said no, it was the work of the devil and she wanted no part of it. Poor dumb me! I wanted to go.

Daddy said he would go with me. "She claims to be in touch with the dead. Well, she doesn't know any of my people, so we shall see," he said. So go we did.

We all sat around a big table. She put a dishpan with some water in the center of the table. Next she brought out a large horn like they used on phonographs at that time. She passed this horn around to each person, so they could see that it had no attachments on it and was open all the way through. After it had been inspected, she placed it in the pan of water and asked everyone to be very quiet. She told someone to please go pull the shades down and turn out the lights. As soon as this was done, she asked us to hold hands with whoever we were sitting by and not to let loose. Her brother and another man decided to sit beside her to see if they could discover any tricks.

Soon pretty lights seemed to be floating around the room, and after a few minutes a voice answered her pleading voice. Inez introduced it as her control spirit. She said a few words to it and then asked who had a friend or relative they wished to talk to.

As the people around the table gave her a name, she would call that name several times, until at last a voice answered.

One voice answered that sounded old and unhappy and seemed to be dragging a heavy chain. "Old Jake," they called him. He started talking and telling us to change our sinful ways before it was too late, and that we wouldn't want to be where he was.

Then, after the control spirit seemed to have a hard time locating him, a young man who had killed himself in the room where Inez had been sleeping started talking. She asked him the questions and he answered:

Inez: Why have you been disturbing my sleep?

Man: Because I want all to know why I did this thing.

Inez: What did you do?

Man: I shot myself.

Inez: Why?

Man: Because of the motorcycle wreck. I was going to die soon anyway. Head injury . . . was losing my mind . . . Don't you remember when I had the wreck with my motorcycle? Soon after, my head started hurting and feeling strange. I went to see my doctor, and he found that I had hurt my head more than we thought and I might need surgery. After I came home I kept feeling worse and decided to end it all.

Please warn everyone never to take their own life. Forgive me.

Then he was gone.

At last Inez asked Daddy whom he wished to speak to, and he said his mother.

So off the control goes to find Grandma.

Then a voice came calling, "Flemmie, Flemmie." I guess she called Daddy that when he was little. Anyway, it went on to say, "I was so sorry to have to leave without seeing you again and the children."

I was so frightened, I don't remember anymore what it said to Daddy. You see, when the voice talked the sound came from that horn that had been put in the pan of water, and the horn would raise up out of that pan and bob up and down in front of the person the voice was talking to.

That voice came in front of me and said, "Jessie, dear, I loved you so much, my first granddaughter. I shall never be far from you. I will watch over you all the days of your life. . . ." That's the last thing I remember, because I guess I passed out.

Next I knew, the lights were on. Inez was in bed, unconscious, they seemed to think, and everyone was talking a mile a minute.

I lay on the couch, listening. They said the young man who had shot himself had been a young farmer who was soon to be married. He had been building a new house and it was nearly done. They remembered the accident but had thought he was doing all right. No one could understand his suicide. He had gone to the room upstairs, and that's where they found him, in the room Inez had slept in. You see, after his death, the house had been sold to Inez's brother.

I have spent many nights in that home and didn't see or hear any ghosts. Inez and her brother were my cousins, and I liked being at the farm with them. I knew the brother of the voice, and he just said that that might explain it.

Daddy and I went home to tell Mama, and Daddy said the voice sounded like his mother and it was scary to listen to it.

Mama said, "Well, you both had better forget that nonsense. Don't fill your minds with trash like that. If it is anything at all, it is the devil," and you know, *I agree with her.*

Inez stayed a few more days. Her relatives were relieved when she announced her departure.

She tried hard to convince them that she was only doing this (whatever it was) to help people. They told her they didn't want any part of it. Then she asked, "Would I deceive my own people?"

I have been told that she was a strange woman and had quite a reputation as a fortune-teller or whatever she called herself, and that farmers and businessmen used to consult her often and claimed great benefits from her advice. Anyway, her own brothers and sisters didn't believe her and didn't like having her around.

I wonder if she had us all hypnotized? It seemed so real. I do hope none of you will ever believe in anything like that. It can only destroy, never help.

She has been dead for several years. She was a very pretty woman, and a wealthy one, too. Wonder what she told St. Peter when she reached the Golden Gate? That's one place her money couldn't buy an entrance to.

Chapter 61

It was the spring of 1917 and all was well in the little town of Lucas, Kansas. Mama was feeling much stronger now. We had good friends and enjoyed being with our relatives, but it was never home to me. It was more like a long vacation; I longed to come back to Manhattan.

I had a young friend, Dan, who was going to college in Manhattan. When the spring term ended, he drove to Lucas to visit us before going on to his home near Wakeeny,

Kansas. He brought me a little diamond ring and insisted that as I was now eighteen years old, we should get married.

He was a farmer, and I didn't agree. I liked being free like the birds.

Mama was very fond of Dan, and when his mother phoned and asked me to come home with Dan for a visit and to meet the family, Mama said I could go.

We started early and arrived late. I didn't like so much country without trees, and there were very few along the way.

Anyway, once there, I had a real nice time. Dan had two sisters, one a few years older — a schoolteacher — and one my age, ready for college. He had several brothers.

The parents came from England, and their customs were different from ours. For instance, the father ruled the house in a stern manner. At mealtime, the food and the plates were all put at the head of the table. The father, after asking the blessing, put the food on the plates, and the mother passed them around to each one, then took her seat at the other end of the table.

I enjoyed going into town with the girls. We went to Quinter, Collier, or Wakeeny. Once or twice a week they took the cream and eggs into Collier.

This was one of the largest farms I had

ever seen. The house was three stories tall and was very beautiful, and they kept it so nice. The only thing wrong was there were very few trees.

I was told by the girls that when Dan and I were married, we would live there, too. This didn't appeal to me at all. I wanted my own little shanty, be it ever so humble. And this mama was too bossy to suit me. I liked her, but I just wasn't used to such strict rules.

I began to decide that I didn't want to be a farmer after all. Anyway, not for a long time yet. It was a nice vacation, and I still have pleasant memories of it.

Mama called one day and said that I had better come home. Daddy had gone to Ft. Riley, Kansas, to work and she needed me. We would plan to move back to Manhattan.

Dan and his sisters drove me to the station and I took the train back to Lucas, promising to come back next year.

Poor dumb me, maybe I should have kept my word and gone back. I imagine the mother was glad I didn't. She probably thought I was a spoiled brat and would never fit in there. I agree, I wouldn't have. I like flowers and trees too much.

Chapter 62

It was 1917, the year that World War I started. Old Kaiser Bill of Germany was on a wild rampage. The USA began drafting the young men, building army camps across the country. Everyone was talking about the war and wondering if and when the United States would become involved.

Daddy had gone to work at the new Quarter Master Laundry in Ft. Riley. His cousin Robert Moore had come to Manhattan from Missouri and had taken the job of chief engineer. Daddy helped him with the machinery and to run the large tumblers used to dry the clothes. It was a big job to keep all that machinery in order.

Our cousin Ray Pauley and many of the young men from Lucas and the surrounding towns had been sent to Ft. Riley for training.

Daddy seldom got back to Lucas now, and when he did, he was always in a hurry. I listened to his stories of all the activity around Ft. Riley and Manhattan, and how both the old and the new laundry were running day and night shifts trying to keep up.

He said to me, "If you were there, I am sure you could get a job."

Of course, I wanted to go right now. He said no. If I had a place to live, it would be all right, but it was very hard to find lodging close to the post. Soldiers were bringing their wives, and they were renting everything available.

He said he would look for a place for me, then I could come there. He wanted a house so we could all move to Manhattan.

Our friend Sarah Anglin's mother lived in Ogden, a small place this side of Ft. Riley. She had let my father put up a tent in her backyard, and he lived there for several months. He did his cooking on an old kerosene stove and had a little camp stove to heat his tent. I said I could live there too, but he said no, it was too cold.

A few days later, we got a letter saying that Aunt Carrie, as we always called her, had said I could come on and live in the house with her, Myrtle, her daughter, and son Edward. I was so happy; it didn't take long to get ready — say good-bye to friends and relatives, get on that train headed for Ogdensburg.

I hated to leave Mama there, but was so anxious to get started earning my own way.

I guess if I had realized what a struggle it would be, I wouldn't have been in such a hurry. As it was, it seemed like that train just crawled along.

At last the porter began calling out, "Ogdensburg, Ogdensburg, don't forget your parcels!"

I hurried off the train, and Myrtle was waiting for me. I was so glad to see her again. I was soon installed in their home and was treated as a member of the family.

Myrtle told me she planned to be married soon; her fiancé was a young soldier. They did a lot of visiting on the phone, as Ogden was off-limits to soldiers. Myrtle didn't work at the Fort.

Chapter 63

Monday morning I was up at six o'clock getting ready to go with Daddy to the laundry to see if they would give me a job. I didn't need to worry; they needed help.

We had to be on the corner of the main street to get on the Interurban streetcar that came from Manhattan and went to Junction City, stopping through Ft. Riley to let the people who worked there off. If we missed the streetcar, we had to walk, and it was a long way. We rode as far as Packers Camp.

All passengers going to the laundry got off, showed their passes to the MP's, and walked across the road and down past a row of officers' homes to the laundry.

Those of us coming to be interviewed for a job were escorted to the building by MP's. We were taken inside a room close by the office and told to wait our turn to be called into the office.

I began to get nervous. I had never been inside a laundry and knew nothing of how the work was done there. In fact, I had never had a good job. I had helped a few farmers' wives in their homes when they had new babies or lots of harvest hands, and I had worked in the little hat shop and the dimestores. This place was so large and noisy, with people every place you looked. I began to worry that they would say I was too small to do the work. I weighed eighty-nine pounds, was five feet two inches, and measured nineteen inches around my waist — still skinny Jessie Lee.

At last I was called to the office and felt better when I saw Uncle Clifford George ready to talk to me. He gave me an application to fill out, so it wasn't so bad after all. I was sure he'd believe I was eighteen; he knew me.

It only took a few minutes. I was sent back to the little room and told to wait there. It seemed like hours, when at last my daddy and another man came for me.

Daddy said, "Well, I guess you get to stay. Do you remember this man?"

I looked at him carefully and said, "No, sir, I don't believe I know him."

So the man said, "No, you couldn't remember me, but I used to rock you to sleep when you were a little baby back in Quick City, Missouri. I had a room at your grandparents' home, and you were there often."

Then Daddy said, "This is Mr. Claude Owens, the boss around here."

Mr. Owens told Daddy to show me around the place and then bring me to the mangle room and they'd find me something to do.

First we went to the back of the place; it seemed like it was a mile long. There were windows all along the sides and a door or two. In the back a big truck was bringing in the dirty clothing. There were women back there sorting them, putting socks in a big canvas basket that had rollers on it so it could be rolled all over the building or to the washing machines. The bath towels and washcloths went into another basket, and so on. A ticket was put on each basket, telling which barracks it belonged to.

Each bundle of clothes was listed with the man's name and number on it. This list went to the checking room with all the slips for that one group. As each piece of clothing was marked, it was easy to find when needed.

After being washed, the clothing was rolled to the tumblers, where they were dried, put back into the baskets, and taken to the mangle room to be ironed, or the shirts to the press room, where ladies stood all day pressing them. Towels and washcloths were folded at long tables. Pillowcases and sheets or blankets were taken to the large mangles to be ironed and folded.

All were placed in baskets with their lot number on them when finished, and wheeled to the checking room to be sorted, tied into bundles, and made ready to be delivered.

This continued load after load all day and all night. The dry cleaning was done at the old laundry down the hill. They were just a short ways apart.

At last I had seen it all and was taken to the folding room, introduced to the girls working there, and shown how the bath towels were to be folded so the number was easy to read. Basket after basket of bath towels came, so hot from the tumblers they would nearly burn your hands.

At noon a big whistle blew and everyone stopped whatever they were doing and rushed to get their lunchboxes, or bought a lunch at the kitchen in the back corner. It cost twenty-five cents back then for soup, sandwich, and coffee.

When that first shift ended, I was so tired I didn't think I could walk back to the bus stop. But I did, and I had to stand up all the way home. Before leaving the building, I was given a temporary pass to use until I could get a small picture taken to be put on a permanent pass.

Chapter 64

The first days were really rough. It took every ounce of determination I could summon to get up those mornings.

Daddy would tell me, "Now, if you want to quit, do it. You don't have to go through all this if you don't want to. You can go back and stay with your mother in Lucas."

For me to admit I couldn't take the long hours of steady work was impossible, so I struggled on. That first month was unadulterated misery. Getting up before the birds, going to work in all kinds of weather, these were things I hadn't even thought of.

My feet were so sore from standing on the cement floors all those hours, I just hobbled along. Someone told me to try some powder called Tiz. I put it in hot water and soaked my feet every night. I don't know if the Tiz did it, or if I just got used to it. I finally could get through the shift in good shape.

I was learning that life is real and life is earnest.

Many people from Manhattan, Ogden, and Junction City were working at the Fort. I soon had new friends plus some old ones who were neighbors before we moved to Lucas.

One morning two new girls came to work. I knew at once I wanted them for my friends. I started talking to them and learned their names were Rhoda and Cora Clary. We soon spent all our spare time together. They lived in Manhattan with their parents.

One day we were told that it was time to start working on the mangles. It took four girls, two to feed the sheets and pillowcases or blankets into the mangle and two more on the other side to catch and fold them. Rhoda and I were partners, and Cora and a girl named Ruth Harold worked together. The four of us learned to work together and became very good at it. We enjoyed it and tried to keep ahead of the others.

As in all places where a lot of people work, many rumors circulated. We now heard through the grapevine that all employees who wanted to keep their jobs would have to take the shots and be vaccinated for smallpox like the soldiers. We heard stories of how sick some people got and how even the soldiers fainted sometimes while taking them. Everyone was dreading it and wondering if it were really true.

Daddy told me he had heard the stories, too, and thought they were true. If I didn't want to take the vaccines, I could give up my job and go home.

I sure didn't want to be sick, but the thought of giving up that nice paycheck was worse, so I said even if we had to take the shots, I would stay. Anyway, it might not be true.

It was. . . .

One morning Mr. Owens came and told

us that all who hadn't been vaccinated or had the shots they were giving for whatever it was (I don't remember), were to line up in a row and pass by a table where some doctors and nurses had their equipment ready. We had our sleeves rolled up, and as we came to the proper spot two nurses, one on each side of us, washed our arms with alcohol. On one side a doctor vaccinated us, and on the other a doctor gave us a shot. It was all over so fast, and we went back to work, except for a few Nervous Nellies who fainted or had hysterics at the sight of the needle. There were several each time this ritual was performed.

I didn't get sick from the shots, but my arm was sore for a day or two. Then my vaccination took. My arm swelled up and got all red and really hurt, but it didn't get bad like so many did. I saw some arms that took weeks to return to normal.

One day Mr. Owens came and called Cora, Ruth, Rhoda, and me together and told us that some men from Washington, D.C., were coming to inspect our laundry and he wanted us to do our very best work. We practiced until we thought we were just about perfect, and when we had to demonstrate those men seemed to think so too. They held their watches in their hands, and in a few minutes one man said, "Wonderful! I have never seen sheets folded as fast or as neatly as these." The two other men agreed. We were proud girls, and after they left, Mr. Owens said he was very proud of us.

When it was time to fold pillowcases we could sit down; that helped a lot. I was enjoying my work now and never felt better. With my ninety-dollar paycheck, I felt very rich.

Chapter 65

Aunt Carrie only charged me four dollars a week to live with her, and that included board and washing, too. Myrtle even ironed my clothes. I saved all I could, and gloated over it, dreaming of the things I would buy when I got time to go shopping. Sometimes we got off at noon on Saturdays if the men were not being shipped out. Myrtle and I would go to Manhattan, and I would buy pretty clothes.

Myrtle and her boyfriend would take me with them often. On Sundays or evenings we often went to Army City or to the guest house, which was about halfway between the gate and Packers Camp. The guest house was called the Hostess House. Myrtle and I would go just to the gate that separated Ogden and Army City. Sid, her friend, would meet us with a cab, we would get in, and away we went to Manhattan or wherever we wanted to go. At the Hostess House we could visit or play games and buy refreshments. We could stay all day on Sundays, if we wanted to.

It was there I met a young doctor, Howard Nichols. He was from Arizona. We quickly became a twosome. He was tall and handsome, with pretty brown eyes and hair. I thought he was wonderful. I still think so. He watched over me almost like my mother did. He called me "Dixie" always. Why, I don't know.

Mama, Tressie, and Lynn wrote that they were doing fine but anxious for spring to come so they could get moved back to Manhattan. Daddy had friends looking for a place for us to live.

All was well with our little world. Sometimes Howard would get a cab and take me to Manhattan, where we visited my aunt Daisy and uncle Bert Frost, or we would go to the movies or to a dance. Then we went back to Ogden. Soldiers had bed check, so they had to be in early. I guess that would be called square. Maybe so, but we enjoyed it. We never had a bottle with us. That was before alcohol became king of the world.

I guess maybe Myrtle was glad when "the Kid," as she and Sid called me, got her own boyfriend and they were free to go by themselves.

Winter passed quickly, and at last a friend called to say they had found a house for rent. It was an apartment house. Two families could live there. We went to see it and rented it at once. It was the big white house at the end of Seventh Street, by the green house where the Moore family had lived. They had sold out and moved to California. The house we rented had been remodeled; we had the upstairs apartment. It was very comfortable.

Daddy took a few days off from work and went to bring Mama and the kids back. Then Daddy folded his tent and came home.

Now it was time for me to leave those dear people who had been so kind to me. How I hated to go, but I knew I should so at last our family could be together again.

Aunt Carrie lived many more years and was always my good friend, and Myrtle has been and still is very dear to me.

Chapter 66

Living in Manhattan meant getting up earlier and getting home later, but it was nice being a family once more.

By this time, the war was getting worse. All the young soldiers were being sent to overseas duty. Brian Pauley, a cousin from Sioux City, Iowa, had come here to enlist. He and our cousin Ray Pauley came to our house whenever they could. They were among the first to go. We missed them so much.

Now we really did have long hours. Up at five-thirty and home after midnight. We worked Sundays and holidays until all the men were shipped out, then we went back to our regular schedule. New trainees came to take their places.

My friend Howard would go with the next shipment. Howard and I decided to get married before he left. We had our plans all made; some friends were going to take us to Westmoreland and we weren't going to tell anyone until we came back. Mama would have a fit.

Howard got the license and went to my house to wait for me. (Big mistake!) It was Saturday and we got off at noon. Somehow Mama got suspicious, and Howard wouldn't lie to her.

When I got home she had convinced Howard how wrong it would be. She said we should wait until he came back and we would have a nice wedding.

I was very upset, but as usual Mama was proved to be right.

In a month Howard was gone — they left on a Sunday. The troop train stopped in Manhattan for twenty minutes. A big crowd was at the depot to see the men and boys off. Tressie and I were there. I can still see that train leaving, with everyone crying and waving as long as it was in sight. That was a very unhappy time.

I went back to work and waited for letters. Sometimes I got two or three all at once, sometimes I got none for days. My friends were great; Rhoda, Cora, Ruth, Tressie, and I went every place together. They had friends on that train, too. Tressie had joined us working at the laundry. We went dancing at the Community House on Fourth and Humboldt. It was a very nice USO then. Such pleasant evenings we spent there. Other times we would get on the Interurban and go to Army City to the dances there. They had very good dances, well chaperoned, and many MP's kept order and the music was good. Army City had boardwalks, restaurants, and a hotel. There was a large hall where relatives and friends could visit with their soldiers, or the boys might bring their girlfriends. It was like the large Hostess House in Ft. Riley. There was a bank, a canteen, a post office, and a dance hall. We only went there on special occasions, and always a crowd of us. No one bothered us. Sometimes we were asked for dates; when we said we would rather go home alone, there were no arguments. The MP's were very strict in those days.

Fall passed into winter and the terrible flu broke out all over Ft. Riley. What a dreadful time that was! People were dying so fast. One day you would be working with a friend, the next day they didn't come to work, and the next report said they were dead.

It went on and on. The soldiers were dying so fast that caskets wouldn't be found for them. We heard that the bodies were being kept in a warehouse until arrangements could be made to send them home for burial.

We were all so frightened, wondering who would be next. As luck would have it, none of our gang had it bad. My sister got it. She was put in a room by herself, and Dr. Clarkson came and gave her medicine. A woman was hired to come and take care of her.

My brother and I were told to stay away. I stayed with Rhoda. Tressie had a light case of it, and none of the family got it.

I followed all the health rules I could and still worried. An entire family who lived in the house I live in today died of it. (Of course, I didn't know at that time it would one day be my home.) Their name was Standish. Our friend Sarah Anglin took care of them.

At last the flu left, as fast as it had come. We could come and go without fear of it.

Chapter 67

1918 was a bad year for me.

We began dreading the trips on the Interurban. Cold winter mornings we would be waiting on that corner, never knowing if the power would go off and we would have a long wait.

Wet, rainy days were even worse. One morning the power was off; a man was waiting at our corner for us. He said the bus wouldn't be going that morning. We were all to go to the Union Pacific depot, because arrangements had been made to take us to work.

When we got there, along with all the others who had waited at the corners along Yuma Street, there was quite a crowd. We were herded into a boxcar on the freight train and hauled to work like a bunch of cattle.

I was so cold, I was sick by the time we got there. I didn't much care whether I lived or died. I had such cramps in my stomach that I couldn't stand up straight.

We had cots in the large rest room, so I was put to bed. That didn't help any. The boss thought I might have a bad appendix. He asked if I had ever had cramps like that before. I never had, so he told me to go to the kitchen and try to get warm.

I sat with my feet in the oven and blankets around me. The cook was told to give me a cup of hot ginger tea. Slowly I got warm again and went back to work.

That was the worst morning. I wasn't the only frozen one. Several were crowded into the kitchen for hot drinks.

Many times while we were coming or going the power went off. Sometimes it might last ten minutes, sometimes an hour. Because so many people traveled back and forth on the Interurban, two cars would be fastened together.

One night it was cold and windy; everyone was anxious to get home. The trolley cars were heated by big stoves. This time we were able to get seats. I was seated across from the stove in the back car.

I told the girl I was sitting with that I was going to go to sleep and not to wake me unless the darned thing tipped over. Well, that is just what it did.

We were just over Stagg Hill. (Anyone going over it today wouldn't believe the horrors of that old roadway, winding around that old hill.) The back coach came loose and started rolling backward. I was just catnapping when someone yelled, "We are going over!" And in less time than it takes to tell, there we were.

I was thrown out of my seat, across the aisle, into a window on the opposite side, missing that stove somehow. (My guardian angel, I am sure.)

My seatmate was lying on the floor, trying to get up. The window was broken.

I had a few cuts on my arm and face. I

had been wearing rimless glasses that fastened in my hair. They were on a chain with a gold hairpin on the end. They were lying on the windowsill, unbroken. I picked them up, opened my purse, which was still on my left arm, and put the glasses in it.

People were trying to get out at the back end. I could hear them talking, but it didn't seem to register. I just lay there like a dummy.

A man yelled, "Hurry up, everyone, get out of here, the damned thing is going to roll on over!"

Still I stayed glued to the spot. Finally some man came back and picked me up, carried me somehow to the back end of the car, and handed me out. I still had my purse. I passed out when they lifted me out of that old wreck.

Next thing I knew, I was in the hospital in a big chair, waiting to be looked at. Well, I waited and waited. Of course, there were a lot of people to be examined. Only one or two were seriously injured. I didn't think I was hurt much, either. When Dan Blanchard, or maybe it was his brother Wearner, came and asked how I felt, I told him fine, I wanted to go home.

He said, "I think you better stay, your face looks bad."

It was numb. I couldn't feel the pain except in my ankle and left wrist. I said, "Please take me home. I will call my doctor."

So he helped me to his car and took me home and managed to get me into the house, where I passed out again.

Things were in turmoil at home. It seems that one of the town busybodies, who would have been on that car except she had taken a day off, had heard about the wreck. She went to the phone and called my mother and told her that the Interurban had tipped over and killed everyone on it.

Mama had fainted and fallen to the floor, where the neighbors found her and were waiting for a doctor to come. Some of them stayed with her, while others got me to bed.

They couldn't find Dr. Clarkson, so at last they got the older Dr. Colt. When he was lifting me up to turn me over, out of my mouth came a lot of blood. He quickly laid me down again. The rest of that night I was just floating in space.

Next morning Dr. Colt came again. I asked for Dr. Clarkson, our doctor, and was told he couldn't come today. Dr. Colt told me that I had a broken right jawbone, some cracked or broken ribs on my left side, and a broken bone in my left wrist and maybe internal injuries besides all the cuts and bruises.

I couldn't move without a lot of pain. I asked Dr. Colt how long it would be before I could go back to work, and he said not for several weeks or months.

It was so hard to talk with that jaw broken; I couldn't get my mouth open enough. My doctor would have told me, "It won't be long if you do as I tell you. You will heal fast!" Dr. Colt told me I was lucky to be alive, I should just be thankful and go to sleep.

I got Tressie to bring a mirror to me, and when I saw my face, I knew what my friend Dan Blanchard had meant. I nearly fainted. Could this creature really be me? Both eyes were black as tar. My face was swollen to twice the normal size. I could only open my mouth a tiny bit, and that hurt so much. My ribs also hurt. I was a mess and the bandages were *so* tight. I was such a scarecrow.

I got angry at myself and my poor doctor. Why didn't he come and tell me I would be well in a few days like he always did? Dr. Clarkson came that afternoon, and I started feeling better just knowing he would get me well soon.

Mama was up again, calling on her reserve strength to watch over me. The doctor said I must not move around for a while or try to get up. No danger of that; I couldn't move around anyway. I sure minded what I was told. Dr. Clarkson was always cheerful and told me I was doing fine, and in two weeks I was up and getting stronger every day. Very stiff and miserable, but up.

I found out my lovely new winter coat I had been so proud of had a torn place. As soon as we were able, those of us who had been hurt went to the owner of the Interurban to see if he would pay the doctor bills. There we ran into trouble. They tried to talk us into forgetting it.

I wanted a new coat. The owner told me to send it to be mended and cleaned and he would pay for that and the doctor bill. That was all, good-bye. . . .

I told him he could have the coat for his daughter. If it was good enough for me, it was good enough for her.

I wonder what he would have done if he had today's bills brought to him. I doubt if all of us together had bills that would be as much as one week in a hospital now.

I don't know how the others fared. I had my coat cleaned and mended, and they did a fine job. I guess the Interurban Company was not in very good financial circumstances.

It was close to Christmas, and I was thinking of going back to work. The first few times I got on that car I was terrified, and Mr. Fisher, the motorman, let me stand beside him until I felt safe enough to take a seat.

Chapter 68

Mama began feeling bad again.

She never got over that phone call telling her about the wreck. I could never stand the sight of that woman again. She lived to be an old lady, and it was impossible not to see her.

My sister had missed the wreck; she hadn't gone to work that day.

It seemed my world was falling apart fast. Things had nearly always gone my way, a few upsets, but nothing serious. Now there were no letters from Howard. I had been corresponding with his mother, and she wrote that she wasn't getting any letters, either. We were worried that he might be a prisoner of war.

Mama grew worse each day. Daddy was working the night shift now. We decided to hire someone to stay with Mama, and the rest of us worked to keep the bills under control.

Before we could find someone to stay with Mama, here came our old standby, Sarah Anglin. She walked into the house and said she would stay as long as we needed her. Her cheerful presence was so comforting to all of us. We knew Mama would get the best of care.

The first of January the doctors told us the time was very short until Mama left us. I couldn't believe it. She had been having bad sick spells as long as I could remember, and she always got better. This time she was just too tired.

About one-thirty A.M. on January 19, 1919, Sarah came to my bed and awakened me. She said Mama wanted me.

I rushed to her and Mama said, "Honey, I am going to leave you now. First I want to release you from the promise you made me. I realize it wouldn't be fair to you, so just forget it."

She had asked me to stay home and try to keep the family together, but she knew I couldn't. My sister had a mind of her own and would do as she wished, and Daddy would look out for Lynn, so I was to take care of myself and keep in touch with the others. She thought I would be going to Arizona to live. The war was ended and the boys would soon be home.

I sat there holding her hand, and soon Sarah said, "I'll get Tressie and Lynn." Daddy hadn't gotten home from work yet.

As soon as Sarah came back with Tressie and Lynn, Mama said, "Oh, I am going now. Good-bye, be good." Then she said, "It is all so beautiful, can't you see these lovely colors?" She was smiling and telling us of the wonders she was seeing. Then, silence.

Sarah said, "She's gone, children. I'll call Dr. Clarkson."

She did. We were too stunned to realize our wonderful mother was really gone.

Daddy came home from work and went all to pieces. Of course, we had known this would happen, but now that it was a reality, no one was ready.

Sarah phoned Mama's sisters. They said they would come when they could. I think they made it by the next day.

Sarah went with us to talk to George Southern, who was the mortician here at that time. He was a friend of Mama's and of her family. He had been their neighbor when he and his family moved to Manhattan. He had played with Grandma's children.

The funeral home was on the south side of Poyntz Avenue, in the 500 block. George was very kind and helped us through this bad time. I still have the bill marked "Paid in full." It was for $139.50. It was $5.00 for opening the grave, and included were two cars for the family.

Mama looked so beautiful lying in her pretty satin bed.

At home we were lost. No matter how sick Mama had been, she always planned everything for us.

Sarah stayed a day or two, then we went back to work. I had always hurried home to tell Mama all the interesting things that happened at work or on a date, and I never left the house without her inspecting me to see if I looked okay. Now I was like a fish out of water. We tried to keep house and work, but in a halfhearted way.

Chapter 69

Early in February I began to feel tired and wanted to sleep instead of going any place. One cold, rainy day we were working at the mangle. The roof had a small hole in it, and water kept dripping on my head. Not a lot, just enough to be annoying. I began to feel hot, then cold.

Rhoda, Cora, Tressie, Ruth, and I had planned to go shopping that Saturday afternoon, then have supper and go to a show. We got home about one o'clock, and I told the girls to go on, I didn't feel up to going.

They left, and I called the doctor, then lay down on the sofa and went to sleep. Dr. Clarkson was in the country with a lady who was having a baby; his office girl said she would send him over when he came back.

I didn't wake up, and the fire went out. When I did finally awaken, I had a terrible headache. In fact, I was just one big ache all over. And freezing. I managed to get some blankets, covered up, and lay down again.

There Dr. Clarkson found me when he finally got there about ten P.M. The house was so cold, and he couldn't get me awake. He called the neighbor next door. Her name was Cora Zarger. She came over and built the fire and put me to bed.

I stayed there the rest of February, all of March, and into April. I had the flu, along with encephalitis. I slept on through it all. No one wanted to come near me. I wouldn't have known if they did.

Then Daddy found a woman who was here from Nebraska looking for work. She said she wasn't afraid of getting the flu, so she came and took care of me. Her name was Lula Wells.

I have no idea how I was kept alive, only what I was told later. One night Cora, our neighbor, stopped the doctor as he was leaving and asked how I was. He told her he didn't expect me to last until morning.

He was wrong that time. Next morning I opened my eyes and looked around. I couldn't understand why my bed was in the living room. The light was on, and I couldn't see anyone there. I wondered if I had been in another accident. I couldn't even lift my hand up off the bed.

At last the door opened and Daddy came into the room, went over, and fixed the fire. I wanted to say something to him, ask him what was wrong, why was I there instead of upstairs in my room? No words would come. Daddy didn't notice I was awake, he just turned and went into the kitchen. I heard voices, then I must have fallen asleep again.

The next time I opened my eyes there was a strange woman walking around, raising window shades and turning out lights. I kept looking at her and wondering if there was something wrong with my eyes; it looked like she was walking with her eyes closed. I thought, No one can do that without bumping into something. I closed my eyes when she came over by the bed and straightened the covers. Soon she left the room.

Daddy came back; I kept looking at him until he noticed I was awake. He rushed over to my bed and said, "Thank God you are awake. You did wake up, at last!" He took my hand in his and started crying and talking at the same time.

I tried to ask about the strange lady I had seen, but no words would come. I couldn't quite manage it.

He went to the phone and called Dr. Clarkson. He came very soon, took my pulse and temperature, and said, "I don't believe it."

He asked me if I was hungry. I didn't seem to know. He ordered some warm milk to be brought in with a spoon, and the strange lady brought it. The doctor put a pillow under my back and gave me a few spoonfuls of milk. He said I was to be given as much as I would take every hour, and he would come back that evening. I was too tired to care if I ate or not.

However, in a few days I began to feel

stronger. I was propped up in bed with pillows. As soon as I could talk I asked Daddy what was wrong with my eyes.

He said, "Nothing, why?"

I said, "Well, it looks like that woman walks around with her eyes closed all the time. No one does that."

He told me not to worry, it wasn't my eyes, it was Lula's problem. The muscles in her eyelids were too weak to hold them up. Then he said that she could see all right.

I felt better after that.

I was so anxious to get out of bed. Lula stayed on; it was good to have her there. She was thirty-two years old, pleasant and kind. She and Tressie got along fine, too. I had a phonograph and some records I liked so much; she would try to keep it going for me.

One day it needed to be turned off and Lula wasn't there, so I decided I could get out of bed and do it myself. It was only a few steps. I got on my feet and started to walk. Down to the floor I went. Lula ran in and helped me back to bed. I was so disgusted with myself.

Soon the doctor told Lula to get me up to sit in the rocking chair every day, for longer periods each time. Next I started walking around in the house, until I had enough strength to stay up all day. I was impatient to get back to work. My friends came by often in the evenings to tell me all the news.

I was just beginning to feel like getting out of the house when the news came telling me what had really happened to my Howard. His best friend, who had been overseas with him, wrote to me, trying to prepare me for what was to come. He told me that Howard had had a rough time. He had been wounded and was in a hospital here in the States and would write to me soon.

I was so happy to know he was safe, or so I thought. Then his mother wrote me that he had more than wounds; he had been where the Germans had used that horrid mustard gas, and his lungs had been so badly damaged that he could only live a short time.

I called her on the phone and told her I would come to that hospital as soon as I could get ready.

She said, "No, my dear, you must not. He doesn't want you to see him or to know how serious his condition really is, so please keep writing cheerful letters, never letting him know how worried we are." She said she would let me know any news she got.

Soon he was gone.

PART III

BETWEEN
THE WARS

(1919-1941)

Chapter 70

I returned to work in June of 1919. I wish I could have erased the previous year from my mind: I felt more dead than alive.

I had a beautiful white satin dress all ready for my wedding. A friend, Mrs. Julia Netson, had made it for me. She did beautiful work and made many wedding dresses. I folded my dress, and with all my beautiful dreams gone, I put it away.

Mama gone, Howard gone — not much to look forward to. But life goes on.

At our house it wasn't home anymore. Daddy grew quieter all the time. My sister had her friends and spent her spare time with them. Lynn stayed with Mama's brother. I sat home like a droopy chicken. I couldn't seem to break through my depression. I guess my illness had been harder on me than we thought. Nothing seemed to matter much; one day was about the same as another.

One picks up the pieces, and being back to work with so many friends around helped so much. We didn't have to put in such long hours anymore. The war was ended, and the young men were coming back to be discharged or to finish out their enlistments. Many of the wives who had stayed to work while their husbands were away were getting ready to go back to their home states. Many were good friends of mine; many I never heard from again.

In August of 1919, the young soldier who was to become your grandfather came back from France, where he had been stationed for a while. He had been reported "missing in action," and his name was on the poster with a gold star after it. There was a large poster in the courthouse for many years with the names of our soldier boys on it. (That gold star remained by his name for years.)

Bill didn't know he was supposed to be dead. He didn't know his family believed he was. He didn't know that the government had sent a letter to his father.

The day he got back, his father was working on Poyntz Avenue, doing some cement work. Bill went to his old home. Strangers there! Seems his father had moved to a smaller house. He finally found someone who told him where his father was working, so he went to find him.

When he came to the place where his father was, he yelled out, "Hello, Dad!"

His father looked up, saw him, and just stared at him. He couldn't believe his eyes, that his son was really standing there.

Of course, Bill, not knowing he was supposed to be dead, thought this was a strange welcome.

At last his dad came out of his trance, and they ended up both trying to talk at the same time to explain the mixup.

His father asked why he didn't write, and Bill said, "I wanted to surprise you."

It wasn't a very happy homecoming for Bill. His mother and two sisters had died while he was gone, all three with tuberculosis. There were two girls and four boys left, Bill, Myron, S.F. (or Bus), and Donald. The girls were Gertrude and Regina. Myron, the oldest son, was married and had a little daughter three years old. The four younger children had been living with sisters of their parents in Wamego. After Bill returned, they wanted to come back to Manhattan, so their father brought them home.

I had never known Bill's family. When we had lived at 1114 Yuma in 1913 they had lived on Colorado Street about the middle of the block on the north side of the street. Bill used to come to our neighborhood sometimes with other kids. I hadn't known him very well. Mama didn't seem to like him much; said she didn't like his ways. I guess she caught him smoking one day. Daddy knew his father; they were good friends, and Daddy had worked with him in the cement work before the war.

After Bill had been home a short time, he phoned one night. He asked if he might come over. I told him no, I was busy.

Daddy asked who had called, so I told him. He asked why I had been so abrupt with him.

I said I didn't feel like visiting with someone I didn't know, I would rather read my book.

"You should have told him to come over. I imagine he's feeling lonely," Daddy said.

I asked why.

Then Daddy told me about the family being so broken up, that his mother and sisters had died while he was away.

I was sorry to hear that, but I didn't want company. I said all right, if he calls again, he can come over.

A few evenings later, he did call again. This time Daddy answered the phone, and over Bill came. And over, and over, and over again. I didn't pay much attention to him and often went with other friends and left him there with Daddy. Still he came back, wanting me to go with him. I tried to get him interested in a girlfriend of mine, but he didn't like her.

One day he begged me to go with him to visit his family, and I went. They were beautiful children, trying to get along as best they could. The youngest, a little boy, was only two years old when his mother died. Marie and Josephine had kept the family together until they took that terrible TB. After they died, their father had no choice except to let his sister and his wife's sister take the children. They did their best to care for them, but the children were homesick. After the mother's death, the father somehow lost their nice home. Gertrude was fourteen when I met them, Regina was thirteen, S.F., or Bus, was eleven, and Donald was six (your great-aunts and -uncles, my dears).

I entered that house, and it was a mess. Never had I seen such an untidy place. The poor kids just didn't know how to manage. It made me sick to see them living like that. After talking a few minutes, Bill and his father had gone to see about some work they were doing, and I told the children that if they would help me, we could clean the old place up. (Their father was a wonderful cement man and bricklayer, but he didn't know how to run a household or manage his money, I found out later.)

I worked hours on that place, scrubbed floors, washed all those dishes, made beds, and dusted. It looked much better.

Then I told them I would fix supper if we could find something. Gertrude said, "Oh, we will go to the store. We can get anything we want, and Daddy will pay at the end of the week." So off she went, once we decided what to get. They wanted breaded pork chops for one thing, a favorite food item of theirs.

We had a nice meal on the table when Bill and his father came back. Afterward we all went to the movies at the Wareham Theater.

I liked those kids. We had a lot in common — we had lost our best friend, our mothers. The father was a kind man and we got along fine. It pleased him that I was taking an interest in his children.

Chapter 71

Bill was at our home more and more. I liked him, but not more than my other friends. I had always gone with tall boys; guess I needed someone to look up to. I was not looking for just one friend, though. I planned to just go on working and staying there with Daddy. He needed me, I thought. Bill was pleasant, nice looking, and lonely — and wanted to get married and have a home. And wanted me to share it. From August until December he was always there.

Here I was, without any plans for the future. I had been happy and contented before losing Mama and Howard. Things had usually gone smoothly, Mama's illness being our biggest problem. Now, with my world turned upside-down, I couldn't seem to take hold of my life again. I had always been anxious to look just right when I went out, and Mama had always looked me over to see that I did. Now I didn't care. I still wasn't feeling too well, after the flu and its complications. I just drifted along.

Bill never gave up; why, I don't know. He could have gone with so many girls. Why me? I was so thin and lifeless, never much to look at. Now I looked like an accident about to happen. But he never gave up. He started telling me how his father would build us a house and began to talk about how nice it would be to have a home and a family.

At last I began to think, Why not? Bill

Jessie Lee Brown and William Foveaux, married December 6, 1919.

won't be Howard, but he is kind, and does need a home after all those years in that terrible war. I thought I could help those children a lot and maybe make a new life for myself, too.

So, one night I said, "All right, I'll go along with you, and we will see what happens." I told him I would do the best I could to make a good home. I also told him I wasn't deeply in love with him, and he decided it didn't matter.

I didn't tell anyone what I was about to do, except Anna, or Ma Campbell, as we called her. She said, "Oh, honey, I wish you wouldn't rush into this. I think it is a big mistake. I have heard that Billy had a bad drinking problem while he was overseas, and you don't need that. Besides, his mother and sisters all died of tuberculosis, and that's a hereditary disease." I told her I would think about it.

That evening I asked Bill about it. He said he had drunk a lot over there, but not anymore. "I don't need it, and will leave it alone," he said.

When I asked about his mother's and sisters' illnesses, he said it wasn't true that they had had TB, and later his father said the same thing. I believed them. The father never did admit it, even after he lost another daughter a few years later to the same thing.

One day I would think all would be well, the next day I wasn't so sure. One Friday Bill came by the house with the marriage license and told me we were going to go to Junction City next morning to be married, by the same man who had married his father and mother. I told him I wasn't ready, but he insisted there was no time like the present. Next day he arrived early with my sister and her friend Arthur Smith, and they were so disappointed that I wasn't ready and waiting.

I don't remember getting dressed, but somehow I did, and off we started. It was a cold, snowy day, December 6, 1919. About halfway there I began to regret my decision and begged them to turn around and go home. They all just laughed and said that all brides get cold feet at the last minute, and kept going on.

We were married by Judge Hurley. I must have said "Yes" at the right times, because soon it was over. The judge gave me a beautiful little white book proclaiming to the world that on this sixth day of December, 1919, he had performed the ceremony.

So much for all my beautiful dreams — no pretty cake, no friends there, no church.

I decided to snap out of it and do my very best to make a good life for us. Bill said we would go over to his brother's and visit them. First we found a nice little café and ate our lunch. Then off we went to meet the brother, his wife, and their little daughter, Maxine.

They were so surprised and seemed very glad that Bill was married. They were so friendly; they insisted we stay for supper, so we did. Their little girl, Maxine, was a beautiful child. I loved her (still do).

After a very pleasant afternoon and evening we returned to Manhattan. Teresa went to a friend's home where she was visiting at the time, and Arthur got on his motorcycle and took off. Daddy didn't care, one way or the other. I guess he liked Bill and thought I was old enough to do as I pleased. He said we were welcome to stay there with him as long as we liked.

Chapter 72

Monday morning I went back to work. I didn't tell anyone I was married. Most of my close friends had married or resigned their jobs by this time, so it was several days before anyone knew I was a Mrs.

Right away Bill started insisting that I resign my work. He said he would make the living. Well, I didn't see how. He was driving a cab at the time and not getting much pay. We needed my money, so I refused.

One day in February, he came home all excited and said he had a new job with his brother at the depot in the Express office in Junction City, and we must move over there real soon.

I was so disappointed to have to leave Manhattan. It was my home and I didn't want to leave it. I cried and I cried, but it didn't do any good.

We went and I hated Junction City. We lived with Myron and Bethel. We paid half of the expenses, and I shared the work with Bethel. We got along fine. We had a room on a floor above theirs, with a long stairway to climb. There was no heat up there. It was so cold and miserable. I had never had to get up and dress in a cold room before, and I hated it. Little Maxine was the nicest part of that time of my life.

The pressure for me to resign my job became so intense that at last I did. I felt so lost and unhappy. I didn't know anyone in Junction City except Myron and Bethel. There were people I had worked with living there, but they were still working.

The days were long; I spent many hours crocheting and tatting. Bethel was the most wonderful housekeeper I think I have ever known. Too good; everything had to be just so. It is hard to live around someone like that.

Chapter 73

I didn't know much about cooking, so Bethel started teaching me. It wasn't long until I started losing my breakfast. After a week or so of this Bethel said, "My dear, I think you are pregnant. You had better see a doctor. I will call ours."

I said no, I would see Dr. Clarkson in Manhattan.

She couldn't wait to tell Bill and Myron.

The next day I took the train and went home. I saw my doctor, and he said Bethel was right, I could expect my little one early in December 1920.

I went back to Junction City, and Bill was very happy. I was, too.

I wanted a family, but not in Junction City. I told them that I was going home to Manhattan and intended to stay there. Myron and Bethel had been wonderful, and I liked them very much, but I didn't want to live with them. So Myron and his friend Mr. Calahan got Bill transferred to the Express office in Manhattan.

I couldn't see any reason why we

shouldn't stay with my father. There was plenty of room. He was away so much, he was no bother. My brother was staying with Uncle Walt, and Teresa and Arthur Smith were now married and in their home. Besides, I liked that house. It was at 1015 Pierre.

We stayed for a few weeks, but Bill wanted to move. So move we did. I couldn't imagine why, but as long as the bills were paid, I didn't care too much. He bought some furniture from a secondhand store, then with what I owned, we moved.

I found out very soon that Bill didn't like people coming by to visit, unless they were his family or old friends. (They were welcome anytime.) He soon gave me to understand that he didn't want my cousin Clyde or other relatives dropping in like they always had.

He was so very jealous of everyone I liked, man, woman, or child. I couldn't understand this. It was my first experience of anyone, except my parents, telling me who I would visit with or what I could and could not do. I didn't like it. I thought he would get over it, but he never did. As long as I followed his rules, all was calm and peaceful.

Anyway, I was so busy getting ready for

my baby and trying to make my home as nice as I could, with the little I had to do it with, that I didn't have time to get lonesome. Bill's father and the children came so often; all holidays and several times through the week they came for meals. I never have really enjoyed cooking, but they praised my efforts, so I tried hard to please all. Later I resented all that extra cooking and cleaning and not seeing anyone except them.

Oh, there were a few exceptions. One couple I liked very much was George and Freda Lundberg. They were true friends all through the years. Both have been gone for several years, and I miss them. George had been in the service with Bill, and they had been friends for years. They were always welcome.

My sister and her husband lived close by and they came over sometimes. We usually walked to the theater on Saturday nights to see the movies. That was our entertainment for the week. I wanted peace above all things, so I didn't argue. I just dreamed of better days to come.

Bill's sister Regina and brother Bus were my favorites. I really loved them, and I was fond of Gertrude. She was a fine young girl, and very intelligent. She was a strong Catholic and resented the fact that I wasn't and didn't want to be. She used to accuse me of cooking meat on Friday because I knew they couldn't have it. That wasn't true; I just didn't think about it. I didn't know all their rules. Just little things like that got on my nerves.

Then Bill decided to move again. This time it was to a nice little house about the 1400 block of Pierre Street. I didn't know anyone in that neighborhood, so the days passed on as before.

About the time I got acquainted with my neighbors, Bill came home and said he had found a house I would like very much and that we would be moved before the baby came. So we moved to a nice little house on Eleventh Street between Poyntz and Houston. I really did like that place and hoped we would stay for a long time, maybe even buy it. The lady who owned it was old and talked like she might sell it. It was October of 1920; the days were still nice and warm.

Daddy had moved to a rooming house. Brother Lynn took care of himself. Teresa and Arthur lived nearby, so I wasn't lonely there. Teresa's husband and his brother Clyde had a sporting goods store and they stayed open late at night. She often stayed there with them. We usually saw them on

Sundays. I also visited Ma Campbell as often as I could. She had promised to take care of me when the baby came. She was a very good midwife and knew just how to manage a home. She gave me a lot of good advice.

Before marriage I had been promised that the fact that I was a Protestant and Bill a Catholic would not matter at all. Now I began to get pressure from his mother's sisters, Aunt Mary Tower and Aunt Francis, as well as his sister Gertrude, to become a Catholic so that the children would be raised in their church.

Well, I couldn't see it. Why couldn't we be friends and believe whatever we felt was right?

At last I gave in and started going to Father Luckey for instructions. How was one raised a Baptist all her life to change to all these new ideas? I didn't. One day Father threw up his hands and said, "I will never be able to convince you, so we may as well discontinue these sessions. I hope you will have your children baptized in our Faith." I told him I would think about it.

Now I want to make this clear to you all. The Catholic people I have known all have been very good friends to me, and if I ever reach the Promised Land, I am sure I shall find many of them there. The same with all the other churches. God didn't say any one of the many churches we have in the world would be the only right one, Protestant, Catholic, or whatever. He said "my church," so I figure anyone who lives up to God's laws the best they can, and trusts and believes in God will find an eternal home someday. We are all sinners and fall short of the glory of God, so let's have respect for all Christian churches and be very careful not to fall into any of these new cults springing up all over these days. Respect of people is what this world doesn't have much of anymore.

I went home after that last lesson and told the family what Father Luckey had said, and that I wouldn't be going there anymore. I was in the doghouse for sure.

Chapter 74

A few weeks later, one cold snowy day in December, I was planning a little dinner party for Teresa, Arthur, George, and Freda to celebrate Bill's and my first wedding anniversary, which would be on Monday. Deember 6. I had worked hard all day Saturday getting ready for the dinner on Sunday evening. I could sleep late Sunday morning; Bill worked nights.

The next morning we had breakfast, then he went to bed and I straightened the house, took a bath, and was feeling fine at noontime.

Soon after, I started having a few little pains that I had never had before. I didn't pay much attention to them. Bill got up and I told him about them, and he got all excited and said that he would call Teresa and Freda and tell them that the party was off.

I said I didn't think it was anything to worry about, to wait awhile. He went ahead and called them anyway, then called for Ma Campbell. She wasn't home, but her son said he would send her over as soon as she returned.

About six o'clock I wished she were there. Dr. Clarkson had been called. I didn't know what to expect; no one had ever told me anything; what to do or what not to do. I knew nothing about childbirth, and I would have died before I asked anyone and let them know how ignorant I was. I expected surgery, and I dreaded being cut open (dumb me!).

There was a knock at the door, and guess who? My dear friend Sarah Anglin came in like an angel of mercy and said, "Well, it looks like I am just in time."

We asked her how she had known we needed her and she said, "I didn't, I'm just checking up on you."

How welcome she was. She had the reddest hair ever and the sweetest smile; she was always in a good humor. She never got excited in times of stress. I felt much better just having her there.

Dr. Clarkson arrived, made examinations, and asked when the pains had started. He said I was doing fine and that it wouldn't be long now. He explained that I was to work along with the pains, and that I should yell as loud as I wanted to.

Ma Campbell came, and got ready to care for the baby.

At 8:10 P.M. I was the mother of an eight-pound baby boy. No knife, no surgery, and I didn't yell. Ma took him to the kitchen to be oiled and dressed. I had been planning on a girl; had her name all ready. Now we had this boy. . . .

I shall never forget the first time I saw that baby. His head was so out of shape, and to me it looked terrible. I yelled, "Take him away! His head is all mashed in."

Then Sarah and Dr. Clarkson started telling me that the baby's head was a little out of shape and would be all right tomorrow. Dr. Clarkson said that Ma Campbell would gently massage it into shape and that I must be thankful that I had a fine and healthy boy.

I didn't believe them, but kept quiet, and sure enough, they were right, his head was all right the next day. I had never seen a new baby before.

I felt good; it hadn't been a half-bad experience. I was anxious to be up and caring for that little boy.

When Dr. Clarkson came to check on us, he asked if he should take the boy with him. I told him not to mention it, he was mine for better or for worse.

Then he wanted to know what we were going to name him. I hadn't planned on a boy's name, so he said he must be named for his father and his doctor: William.

I didn't like that much, but when we added Joseph, I said all right, and I called him Billy Joe. Soon everyone did.

Ma Campbell took wonderful care of us. She cooked, cleaned house, and did the laundry all for $15 a week. She stayed for two weeks. Our doctor bill was $20.

Aunt Teresa and Uncle Arthur came to

see their new nephew. George and Freda came with their little daughter, who was a month old. What a happy time it was. Bill was so proud of that baby, and the plans we made for him were wonderful.

Grandpa Henry and the children came and brought, of all things, a fine new high chair. Bethel and Myron and little Maxine drove over from Junction City. Maxine was so excited; she kept holding the baby's hand and looking at him.

She said to me, "Her is a him, ain't she, Aunt Jess?"

She was the sweetest little girl, she wanted to hold the baby. Her mother helped her, telling her this was a real live doll. Maxine called him "doll baby" for a long time.

Chapter 75

I was well and busier now than before. That baby was the nicest thing that had ever happened to me. I adored him. I enjoyed every hour of the day; even getting up at night didn't bother me. I dreamed of all the things I would do for him. He grew so fast and was healthy, bright, and happy.

The neighbors began coming in often.

Next door lived a family named Compton, a widow with one daughter.

Across the street were Charlie and Maude Miller and their two children, Thelma and Jack. Thelma was eighteen years old, and Jack was nine. Charlie owned a barbershop on Poyntz Avenue (where Pete Peterson's shop was for so long). They were fine neighbors and loved Billy Joe. They took care of him often so I could keep up with my housework. That was a great help to me.

On the corner of Eleventh and Houston lived Joe Burr, his mother, and sister Esther. Bill and Joe had played ball on the same team and were friends. I knew him from school days; he had teased me unmercifully. He was one of the boys who always asked me if I had rocks in my pockets on windy days. He called me Jessica. He liked children and came to see Billy Joe when he could. The neighbors were all so nice to us.

I was happy and contented, until out of the blue Bill announced that we were moving to the north part of town, Fourth and Laramie. That old house was replaced long ago, but I'll never forget it — what a mess. I didn't see it before we moved, as usual. I was told it had a cheaper rent. It was a double house; we moved into the east side. How I hated that place! It had four small rooms, no bath, just a stool in a cubbyhole off the kitchen. It had old splintery bare floors to scrub. It was December 1921; Billy Joe was one year old. That place was so cold and miserable.

The only thing that made that place bearable was the fact that my good friend Myrtle Wood Hamilton and her children were living in the other part of this mansion. Her husband, a soldier, was away at the time. She hated it, too.

Why we had to move there, I couldn't understand. It sure wasn't a place for a baby. I don't think a rat would have wanted to live there. We stayed until February 1922. It was only a short time, but it seemed a long, long time to me.

One day Bill went to town to get a haircut, and Charlie Miller told him that they had moved into a double house on Eleventh and Houston, and that the front apartment was still for rent. He asked Bill to rent it. It was only a half block from where we had lived before, so Bill rented it from Charlie. He hurried home to tell me to get ready to move again by the end of the week.

This time I was happy to obey. I hated

to leave Myrtle there, but she would leave it, too, when her husband came home. Myrtle and I have often talked about that winter in that old house that was falling down, with no one to fix the windows, no one to fix the roof.

This house on Houston Street was warm and comfortable. We burned coal for fuel; it was dirty, but it made fine fires. Now happy days were here again.

It was nice being with Maude and Thelma again. Billy Joe enjoyed all the attention he was getting from them. Thelma soon married John Harner and moved to Keats or Riley, Kansas. But, she came home often.

In the same block a young girl, Marie Hays, lived with her parents, Mr. and Mrs. Cap Hays. She often took Billy Joe for long rides in his carriage. She was a teenager and was a big help to me. She was a sweet girl. She later married a Mr. Everett Bishop and moved to the country. I didn't see her again for several years. (Yesterday she came to see me, and we talked of those days when we were neighbors, and she told me how much she had enjoyed taking my baby for long walks and dreaming of wheeling her own children in their carriages, and how she never got to because they were living in the country.)

I wasn't feeling too well, as I was expecting another child. It was nice having Esther Burr for a neighbor; she was a nurse and gave me a lot of good advice.

Then in May Bill announced that we were moving again. He said he had rented a little house on Colorado Street, number 925, and we could live alone. He didn't like living in the same building with other people.

We moved. I was getting good at it. I liked this little house, and the neighbors were good, friendly people.

Chapter 76

Dr. Clarkson told me to expect this child in June, about the twelfth or fifteenth. June passed. Also part of July. The doctor had to go away to a convention and was going someplace else to visit family or friends, so he asked Dr. Reitzel to be my doctor while he was gone.

Dr. Reitzel came to see me. (We seldom went to a doctor's office in those days, or I didn't, anyway.) He decided I was going to have twins.

July was a hot, dry month. We spent most of our spare time on Hunter's Island at my aunt Louise and uncle John Hunter's home. My aunt Louise had been a great comfort to me since Mama had been taken away, and Bill liked them, too. It was nice on the farm.

August came. I was so miserable, I could only shuffle along. Once on a chair, I had to stay there until someone helped me up. Regina was there part-time, and a neighbor, Delia Thompson, was a lot of help too.

Dr. Clarkson returned from his trip and was very surprised to find me still waiting. By this time I couldn't step over the doorsill, so I had to stay in the house. I hadn't had shoes on for weeks, so there I was, barefooted in my old kimonos, a miserable sight to behold.

It was a miserable time for all of us. My friends were sure I was going to die, so they only stayed to talk a few minutes. They told me later that they didn't know what to say to me, they were so sure I was done for this time.

I wasn't so sure myself that they weren't right. I can't remember anyone, not even my doctor, mentioning the hospital. Wonder why?

I had no one to stay with me this time. I

had waited too long. Ma Campbell's daughter-in-law Emma was due to deliver her child any time, so Ma had to be with her. I don't blame my other friends. I don't think I would have wanted to be with someone I was sure wouldn't live, either, at that time. I have long since learned that that's the time one *is* needed, when the chips are down.

Well, I was lucky. Emma's baby arrived and mine lingered on. One morning Ma Campbell called and said she could come any time now that I needed her.

It was as if I had been waiting for her. On the twelfth day of August 1922, that contrary child decided to come into the world.

Dr. Clarkson sure earned his money that night. I think he was as exhausted as I was when it was all over. He said, "My goodness, what a big fellow! Hurry up, Anna, and get him ready to be weighed." He weighed thirteen pounds, looked like he was three months old, had long brown hair, and his fingernails and toenails were unbelievable. The first thing they did was to get rid of them.

He was a good baby. That was a blessing because it was all I could do to lift him. I named him Francis Sylvester, after his uncle Bus.

I was slow getting over this birth, and it was so hot that August. Imagine me trying to take care of this little one and a year-and-half-old boy who could run like a deer. I kept the screen doors locked to keep Billy Joe from getting away. Such a summer it was.

Chapter 77

Then guess what? We moved again.

This time it was upstairs over the barbershop. It was a nice apartment, and Bill's sister Regina was staying with us.

We enjoyed watching the people moving along the street below. Ferelman's Market was next door, very handy. We would take the babies and go to the afternoon movies.

In the spring of 1923 we moved back to 925 Colorado Street and lived there until fall. I was ready to have another baby the latter part of August.

Bill received a bonus for "overseas duty" from the state or government, and we looked for a place to buy. I wanted to stop this confounded moving.

I wanted to find a place on the south side

of Poyntz Avenue. But Bill, who now delivered groceries for Brown's Grocery Store, heard about this place (where I still live now). He had it all arranged for before I knew it. I never even saw it until moving day. Well, he made the down payment, I signed the papers, then we paid the bills we had and called the moving van for the last time. Just six weeks before Duane — or Chick, as we call him — was born, we moved in.

Bill's sisters Gertrude and Regina took the children to their home to care for until we could get the place ready to live in. If I had seen it beforehand, wild horses couldn't have dragged me into that filthy place. Never before or after have I seen anything like it. The floors were full of grease and dirt and so splintery in the kitchen. When I saw the yard I nearly fainted, and when I got inside all I could do was cry and scream, "I won't live here! No human could get this place clean. I won't live in a pigpen, and you can't make me!"

After my hysterics, I started looking around. I found two bedrooms, almost as dirty as the kitchen. Then a living room and a dining room. Between the living room and bedroom was a double doorway, with big round columns. I didn't like that, but since I wasn't a carpenter, I didn't see any way to get rid of it at that time.

The door between the living room and dining room had huge scratches on it. All the doors had scratches where those dear dogs had clawed them. At one time the doors had been varnished, but now they were so filthy dirty, they were black.

There was chewing gum everywhere. It was stuck on walls, woodwork, any place you might look. The boards above the door were all loose and sagging where lines had been stretched to dry clothes on. Some of the cord was still hanging.

The wallpaper was hideous. It had large dark figures and was all colors. There were great chunks hanging loose on the kitchen and bedroom walls. In the kitchen there was an old sink. We had city water, but on a shelf beside the sink was a pump for cistern water. It was a horrible, rusty-looking thing. That had to go! The pantry, aside from the dirt, wouldn't be bad with some paint.

The cistern was under the bathroom, and had a trapdoor. I was told the dear people who had lived there before had used it as a refrigerator, that they had put their milk and butter down there. They had large nails in the wooden boxlike structure surrounding it. Well, there would be no more of that. I'd get that done away with some way, or

Daddy Henry would. The tub and stool were stained from iron in the water.

The first thing was to scour those bedrooms and get the beds up. Bill had the day off, and two of his friends came and helped us all day. By evening we had the floors all scrubbed with some very strong preparation that smelled clean and made me feel better.

We got the stove up and enough dishes unpacked so we could manage to exist. One strange thing: we never found a bedbug or a cockroach anyplace.

We prepared a lunch, then went after the boys and came home to spend the first night in my dream house. Ha, ha, ha.

323 Thurston Street, where Jessie Lee has lived since 1923.

Chapter 78

The next day my sister came and we scrubbed windows and woodwork, put up window shades, and little by little got by until Duane was born on October 25, 1923. Dr. Clarkson and Ma Campbell were there again. All went well and Duane was born while the doctor was reading the paper. He wouldn't believe me when I told him he was needed; he said I had lots of time yet. Was he surprised when that baby cried! Ma arrived soon and took charge. Duane weighed eleven pounds and was a beautiful baby.

Three children are a little more work than two. It's a good thing they were strong and healthy. As soon as I was able to manage things, I started planning on getting that awful wallpaper off those walls and ceilings.

I called Mr. Thompson. He was our neighbor when we lived on Colorado Street and was a paper hanger and painter. He came and looked the place over and told me that if we got the old paper off, he would paper the walls and paint the woodwork and lay some linoleum for me.

I asked him how in the world I could get that paper off and he said it would be a hard, messy job. I would have to fill a tub with hot water and take rags or soft brushes or anything I could find to use to get that water on the paper until it was soaking wet. Then I had to take large putty knives and scrape the paper off.

It seemed hopeless, but where there is a will there is a way. Room by room we took that paper off. Some places there were six and seven coats and it stuck like glue. At last it was done. I cried a river of tears that year.

Mr. Thompson brought a sample book of wallpaper and we selected pretty paper for all the rooms. He painted all the woodwork and put that paper on the walls and linoleum on the floors. I got curtains for the windows and was so proud of the place. It was easy to keep clean now. I really started living again. We never had more than enough money to cover our expenses, but we were healthy. The house payments were small and we were doing as well as the average family.

In February 1925 little Marjorie Lee came along. We weren't expecting her after three boys.

This time the birth took me by surprise.

We had company all evening — Myron, Bethel, and Maxine had come over. They left about eleven and I was straightening up the kitchen when suddenly I knew it was time to call Ma and the doctor.

I called Bill. He did the phoning and I had just gone into the bedroom when I felt that child was going to fall on the floor. Dr. Clarkson came rushing in. He remembered how fast Duane had arrived, and he wanted this to be different. He was just in time, and he didn't even take off his overcoat. He just pushed up his sleeves and caught that child while instructing Bill how to lift me into the bed.

He looked so funny, his hat pushed back on his head, standing there in his overcoat, holding that tiny infant. The more he told me to keep quiet, the more I giggled. He threatened to spank me hard if I didn't stop.

Ma got there and took over. Under her capable supervision we soon settled down. My little girl didn't weigh but five pounds; she was so tiny and fragile. She wasn't so strong as the boys were, but we managed to bring her through that first year. Then she got stronger. They were all good babies, but the four of them took every minute of my day. There was so much washing, ironing, cooking, and cleaning.

Chapter 79

About this time Bill began to go to the American Legion with some of the fellows he had been in the army with. I didn't mind; I thought it was good for him to go someplace once in a while. I was so busy that I couldn't go.

One night two of his buddies brought him home and helped him into the house. He was very sick. They told me not to worry, that he had eaten something after the meeting that made him sick and he would be all right in the morning. I let them put him to bed and I was so sorry that he felt so bad. He went to sleep and so did I.

Not long after that it happened again. I was worried this time and wanted to call Dr. Clarkson. They said not to, they were sure he would be all right, so I got cold cloths for his head and sympathized with him. He seemed to feel so bad.

I began to wonder what kind of food they served at that place, so I mentioned it to my neighbor Ethel Scritchfield and she said, "What time did they come home?"

I said, "Oh, way late, after one o'clock."

Ethel said, "My dear, the meetings are over way before that. Bert went and he was home soon after ten o'clock." Then she told me that after the meetings some of the men went to find some liquor. She hoped that wasn't the case.

Now I had never seen a person under the influence of alcohol. I knew Mama had a brother, my uncle Jesse, that used to drink. If we were at Grandma's when he was home from one of his bad times, we were told to stay away from his room and play away from the house and be careful not to wake him, that he was sick. Mama had told me about it when I was older. She said that the family felt so ashamed about his drinking like that.

I thought about what Ma Campbell had told me, how terrible it was to live around an alcoholic. I prayed it wasn't true, that Bill was starting it again. But it was true, Old King Alcohol took over in 1925, or started to.

Now, my dears, I am afraid that all through the years I have given you a very bad image of your grandfather. I must in all fairness try to explain to you why. You will wonder why I am telling you all these things. I want to try to show you what can

261

happen to a family if either the mother or father becomes an alcoholic.

Your grandfather was a quiet, nice-looking man, a hard worker, and until then a good husband. I had no major complaints. I didn't like his jealousy, and wished he liked more of the things I did — but all in all he was a very decent person. As honest as could be. He had no sense of the value of money, but gave me his money and I paid the bills. He was kind to me as long as I did what he told me to.

I was too busy taking care of my little ones to argue. He resented the time I spent with the children. When he was home he wanted me to have everything under control and pay attention to him. He was strict with the children and taught them to mind and not to talk back to their mother. I appreciated that. Sometimes he would go for weeks and never go anyplace, only in the neighborhood.

We had fine neighbors, and we started having card parties at each other's homes. We all enjoyed those evenings. I loved to play pinochle. We had prizes for the best players, and a nice lunch was served after the games. Bill enjoyed this for a long time, too. Ruby Colony, a young neighbor girl, used to come here and do her homework and be with the children when we went to play cards.

Then Bill started going to meetings again and coming home from work with his bottle and insisting that I join him. He always wanted to start singing after a few drinks. I'd refuse and he would get angry. The next day he was so sorry, he'd say it wouldn't happen again. Then there would be another period of staying home.

Chapter 80

It was now 1926 and Arthur Merle came to join the family on April 27 of that year. It was a very windy day. I washed clothes, and it was hard to keep them on the clothesline. I baked cakes and cookies, visited with a neighbor awhile, then went out to bring clothes in. Mrs. Orville Gilman, the woman who lived next door, asked how I was. She thought maybe this wind might blow a little bundle my way. I told her no, I was fine, and that I planned to get my ironing done in the afternoon. She told me to rest awhile. I went inside to get lunch ready.

Bill had started working at construction

jobs and did well. He was hauling sand by our house, and the children would stand at the window watching for him. He would slow down and wave to them.

After lunch I washed the dishes, put the children to bed for their naps, and felt fine.

Suddenly I had a pain I recognized. I called Ma and told her to hurry. She was here in twenty minutes, and at one-thirty, so was Merle. No trouble at all.

Ma took care of us and then called Dr. Clarkson. I hadn't bothered to tell him I was expecting this time. In fact, I was a little angry with him. I had asked him to tell me some way to stop having so many children so fast, and he always insisted he didn't know. He said I was the type who should have them. I had such beautiful healthy babies and I gave birth so easy, and I seemed healthy, too. I never did like him quite so much after that because I didn't believe him.

Now he was surprised when he came in and saw the baby all dressed and sleeping. He looked us over and complimented Ma on a job well done. He told me to prepare him for the shock next time and that he would come by the next day to see how we were doing.

That night Ma got a call that her daughter in Kansas City was very sick, and she had to go. She called my cousin Lily Moore, and she said she could stay here daytimes, so another problem was solved.

That night Bill arrived on time and was so glad to see another boy, number four. We explained about Ma having to leave, and Lily coming the next day, and that we would have to manage alone that night.

All went well. Bill left early for work the next morning and Lily came. She was one of the sweetest women ever to live on this earth. She was so good, and the little ones liked her so much. She loved Duane best. He was so cute. She said she would never forget how he always asked her to be careful when she washed his hands because he had sores on them. He always managed to cut or scratch his little hands some way.

The next night Lily waited supper for Bill, but he didn't come. She was anxious to leave, so I told her to go on. I was sure he would be home any minute. She had given the children and me our supper, and I told her that Billy Joe could do anything I needed done. He was five years old and could really help a lot.

One hour passed, no Bill. I didn't know what to do. At that time new mothers were supposed to stay in bed nine days, and here

I was with a baby one day old and four more needing to be put to bed. So I got up, and with Billy Joe's help we got them all to bed.

I was worried because a storm was coming. That's the one thing I feared most. It had been warm that day, and some of the windows had been opened and Lily had forgotten to close them. I got up again and closed them.

Then the baby wanted his bottle, so I went to the kitchen and got that ready, put him in my bed, got in, fed him, and fell asleep, too exhausted to know it was storming.

Morning came. It was a beautiful day, but still no Bill. Lily came, fixed breakfast, cared for the children, then came to talk to me. She asked if I had noticed how hard it had rained and how sharp the lightning had been.

I told her no.

She said she had remembered she had left the windows open in two rooms, but she knew Bill would close them.

Billy Joe said, "No, Mama did."

She asked, "What?"

Billy Joe told her that Daddy hadn't come home yet.

She said, "You mean you got out of that

bed and walked in those rooms?"

I said, "Yes, what would you have done? I also changed the baby, fed him [He was on Eagle brand milk formula, as all mine were. It was easy to prepare. It was warmed by putting the bottle in a pan of hot water.], then I went to sleep. That's why I didn't hear the storm."

She insisted I must not stay alone again, and when the doctor came she told him what I had done. He said he didn't think it had hurt me.

That evening Bill showed up on time. He made no mention of his overnight delay. Lily didn't say anything. Neither did I.

He began doing all he could to help. After she left, he was again so sorry. He had met friends after work and they took a drink, a toast to the new son. And then another until they ended up at the home of one friend.

He got home every night for at least two months after that.

Each time he went on one of these little sprees I lost respect for him. I couldn't imagine anyone not being able to stop anything that harmed themselves and others.

Chapter 81

Now with five little ones I had to wash every day, sometimes twice. I had no time for neighbors, phone calls, or outside contacts with relatives or friends.

Bill's folks didn't come here so often now. Regina had married and was having one child after another, too. We had a lot in common those days; her husband drank, too. We got together when we could.

Gertrude had gone into nurse's training in a Catholic school and had just finished when she came down with TB. She was taken to Norton, Kansas, and died there. She had the same kind her mother and two sisters had.

Now I had another fear, that my children would get TB. They were precious to me, and I'd fight to the death to protect them. I was so proud of them.

I had another battle every time I sent the children to Sunday school. They went with the neighbors. Bill didn't have nerve enough to tell the neighbors the children couldn't go with them, but he tried every way he

Arthur Merle (Mudd), age 5; Faye Marie (Sadie), age 4; and Marjorie Lee (Margie), age 6.

could to stop me from sending them. He made fun of our churches, told the kids everything they learned there was wrong. I sent them anyway. Bill seldom went near his church. Since I had known him he had only gone a few times with his brothers and sisters, that's all.

My days were full to the brim. I was up early in the morning and to bed late at night. I began to look and feel like something the cats dragged in. I had no interest in anything but my children.

Then fourteen months after Arthur Merle's birth my little Faye Marie was born. She was a doll, six pounds of energy. She had blue eyes and golden hair.

Now I had two daughters, one with pretty auburn hair and blue eyes and my little blonde.

The Sunday she came was a very trying day. In the afternoon my sister and her husband, Arthur, came and we all had supper which Teresa and I cooked. They now had a beautiful little son, just about Marjorie Lee's age. I was very fond of him; he played with my children a lot.

Arthur had brought his bottle along. After supper the men went to the back porch and kept drinking. When they drank, they got very hard to get along with, and the children were afraid of them. They would be punished for no reason at all.

About this time I started having pains. Teresa called Ma and she came.

Such a night we put in! Bill and Art suddenly knew just what to do, even though they could hardly stand on their feet. Ma asked them to please stay outside and allow us a little privacy. Teresa attempted to get Art to go home. No luck. She told them they must stay out of the way so Ma could do what needed to be done. It went on and on. I felt worse and worse, I was so nervous. I didn't know what I was about. It was after midnight when sis finally got Arthur started home. She had to drive, and poor little Bobby was so scared.

Soon as they left all went well. Bill passed out on the porch and we were alone at last. Ma had known about these drinking spells for a long time, but God bless her, she never once said, "I warned you."

Little Faye Marie was there at last after all the commotion. We had had to lock the doors to keep those two drunks out. Ma stayed with me a week, then had to go help someone else.

Chapter 82

Now things really got bad. Bill and his drinking buddies were getting worse all the time, staying away from work, spending paychecks before coming home.

What was it all doing to me? It was changing me from a happy-go-lucky character into someone not nice to know. I began to think of all of them as Enemy No. 1. I became resentful and full of hate. Each time I had to tell someone I couldn't pay a bill, I died a little. I was so ashamed, even of my name. I thought everyone was talking about me and my problems, and I started avoiding everyone. Only the friends who had the same problems did I see. Times were very bad now, and I could see no reason for it. All I asked was food and clothing. We had less and less all the time.

Billy Joe started kindergarten, then first grade. He liked to go to school. I had taught him his ABC's and to count before he started.

I now had six children, and the oldest lacked three months of being seven years old.

I wasn't a wife, I was a darned slave with no pay. I became so full of hate for that husband of mine, only God above kept me from killing him. I know I wanted to.

I wondered what in the world I could do to better conditions. I became distrustful and angry with the world.

I now thought of the children as all mine. They were my responsibility. Somehow I had to manage to keep them fed and give them something to wear. I had bought insurance policies and had several small ones on myself that had been taken when I was a youngster. I started cashing one when I was desperate, then taking another to replace it. I had managed to get small policies on each child and had insurance on the house and its contents. Those had to be paid above all else. Those policies were wonderful; they kept us from starving.

When Faye Marie was a year old, I began to wonder what I could do to start earning some money. I started selling products for the Newton Company of Newark, back East. I took orders for cosmetics, spices, and extracts.

It was fun and I enjoyed it. It meant getting up earlier in the morning, but it was something to do. There was a lot of walking. I had a large baby carriage, so I put

Arthur Merle and Faye Marie in it along with my sample case. With the others walking along, I'd walk the streets, taking orders. Then when the goods arrived, I had to deliver them.

I did quite well with this, so I added Fashion Frocks to my business. They sent me free dresses, and the Newton Company sent me many nice prizes.

Elmer Holbert, who kept the little grocery store on the corner of Third and Thurston, gave me some work. He was a very kind-hearted man who had been a friend to Mama's family for many years and had served in the army with my uncle Jesse. I did laundry for him and his son, who lived with him and went to school. Two afternoons through the summer weeks he would have me keep the store while he went to his farm to work in his garden. He would come back happy, with a load of fresh fruit and vegetables. He gave me a lot of them and paid me with groceries.

He was good to the children, too. He had no use for Bill because of the booze. I could bring the babies and let them sleep in the back room, so the summers worked out fine.

Winter was a different story, but with the help of another friend and neighbor, I got

Grandson Ray Rutledge (with a neighbor's daughter) takes a ride in the baby carriage, just as his mother, Sadie, did when Jessie Lee was selling goods door-to-door.

some shirts to iron for the college students. She and her husband went for them and took them back when I was finished. I had to give up on the other work; it was too cold to walk and take the children out.

Chapter 83

The 1930s were hard to live through.

I'll always remember the terrible dust storms; the wind blew hard for days. That dust could get in no matter what one tried to do to prevent it.

The three oldest children were in school now. About noon one day someone at the school called and said, "The storm is getting so bad we will have to close the school until it gets better. Please send someone after the children, it isn't safe for them to be outside."

Bill had just got home for lunch, so he took the truck and went after them. The dust was every place, on the beds, the table, dishes. And the food tasted gritty, no matter what one did to protect it. It was hard to breathe. Many people had what they called "dust pneumonia." Never again has this happened, and I hope it never will.

Bill straightened up for a while. We visited some friends, he worked, and we got straight with the world again. I tried to treat him all right and began to think that maybe now that baby Faye Marie was ready for kindergarten he would change for good.

Where was my dad these days? He never felt welcome in our home, so he only came to see me when he knew Bill was not there. Back at the time Billy Joe was born, Daddy had been in Missouri visiting his sisters and friends. He was so happy to have a grandson, he hurried home when he could.

He had only been at our home two days

when Bill asked me, "How long does your old man plan to stay here?"

I told him I thought a few days.

He said, "That better be all. This isn't a boardinghouse."

I told him my dad was as good as his, and if mine wasn't welcome, neither was his.

Dad, who had been coming from his room, overheard what Bill had said. He turned around, went into his room, and packed his things. As soon as Bill went to work, Daddy told me he had heard him talking to me and was on his way. From then on Daddy stayed away from Bill.

Daddy worked and managed very well looking after himself. One day he was hurt in a car wreck. After he was able to be up and around he took a job at the Odd Fellows Home, where he remained until he died in 1941. He was loved and respected there, and the residents mourned him when he suddenly died.

To go back to the Thirties — work became scarce. Construction slowed down, the banks failed . . . Then Bill started drinking again. How I hated him! The WPA and Commodities that came next were complete humiliation for me. I hated having to sign up for those food gifts. I had no choice. I couldn't let my children starve, so I signed the form and accepted the food. That was the hardest thing I had had to face up until then.

I couldn't force myself to go for them. Billy Joe was twelve years old now. He had a friend, Barney Fereleman, about fifteen, and his father still had the grocery store. Barney would get the delivery wagon and he and Billy Joe would go and get the supplies for our family.

Bill wouldn't go for them, either; he didn't have the nerve. If I hadn't been so hate filled and proud, I would have been so very thankful. Instead I resented the fact that they were doled out to the poor and those too dumb to earn a living. I didn't quite believe no work existed. The only excuse for not working that I could see was illness. I was wrong. It was true, there was no work.

My neighbors were suffering the same as I was. We received from the supply room at the courthouse two sacks of flour, sugar, lard, powdered milk, rice, prunes, canned mutton, and other things. I thought I'd never be able to use all those prunes. Then I thought about canning them. I did, and they were very good. All the food was good. Now I know how foolish I was.

Chapter 84

Bill was behaving well again. He started getting small jobs here and there. Then in 1934, when Faye Marie was nearly seven, we had another baby. The Lord must have felt sorry for me to have spaced them that far apart.

I didn't tell Dr. Clarkson. He had always told me to call him if he was needed. I had a few times when the children were sick, but he usually told me what to do after I described their symptoms. I wasn't going to have a doctor bill that wouldn't be paid.

I went on as usual working from early morning until very late at night. I stayed home and no one knew my secret but me, only the neighbors, my sister, and Regina. I began the same pattern as with Francis. I became more silent and secretive all the time. I really didn't care whether I lived or not, thought it might be best if I didn't. I knew I was going overtime again, waiting too long for the baby — old kimonos and no shoes.

One day Dr. Salley, a young doctor who,

with his wife, had lived in an apartment at my sister's home, came to the back door to ask the boys if they had any fishing worms so he could go fishing.

He looked at me and asked if I was all right.

I said I guessed so.

He said he didn't think so and asked what my doctor said.

I told him that I didn't have any.

He said, "You do now. Call me when you need me."

I told him I couldn't because there was no money to pay him.

He said to never mind about that. He had work that Bill could do, and he'd see that Bill did it. He asked a few more questions and said, "I think you are overtime now. Let's set a date for Saturday morning. I'll come over and if all's well, we'll see if we can't hurry this along." He got his fishing bait and left.

He returned Saturday morning, June 29, and after an examination, he gave me a shot of some kind. I had made arrangements for the children to stay with a neighbor, and another was ready to come over.

No Ma Campbell this time; she had died after a short illness. (I am sure she is in heaven now.)

That shot did the work, and by ten-thirty on June 29, Marion Myron was here, a big ten-pound boy.

My friends and neighbors came and cared for him. The doctor left medicine for me and went home.

I was feeling fine. I had some hemorrhaging, but I had pills for that. Billy Joe was now fourteen and my right hand. He looked after the other children and helped me a lot, too. All of them had their chores. One Billy Joe had that he hated was to get up and start the fires on cold mornings. We had a little coal house on the alley. The children carried in the fuel.

Nighttime came, and no Bill. We soon learned that he was in the jailhouse after a drunken brawl in a café someplace, sentenced to ten days.

It was a relief not to have him around. Food was scarce. My father was still alive then, and he came by and brought money to buy the Eagle brand milk for the new boy and a few other things. Bill's dad brought food, too. The neighbors helped keep the work done.

It was so hot. August was at its worst that year. I took care of the baby there in bed, giving him his bath and clean clothes before anyone got there. Billy Joe did the cooking (anyway, he tried).

The chief of police came up. It was Arthur Schleen, an old childhood friend. He asked me if I wanted him to send Bill home, that Bill had promised to behave.

I told him, "No. Keep him forever, as far as I'm concerned."

He said, "No, I can't do that, but we'll let him cool his heels awhile."

When he did come home, oh, he was so sorry, never again. Well, I had learned long ago how sorry he was. Just until he took a notion to celebrate.

I thought it was just pure meanness, and I was going to get even. A little voice started saying to me, " 'Vengeance is Mine', saith the Lord." Then I'd think, "Then why doesn't He do something?" I began to think they should declare a bounty on drunks like they did coyotes. They were no earthly good to themselves or anybody else. This man had ruined my life and I was going to get even some way.

Chapter 85

Marion was a great joy to all of us, and the most meddlesome of the gang. He learned to open the drawer where we kept the bread and he would have all the inside pulled out by the time we found him. Or he'd open the icebox and pull something out on the floor. He was just walking good in 1935, and I was going to have another baby.

Great grief, would it never stop? I'd say, "Dear Lord, why me? All these people with money enough to raise them right, and you know I can't do what I should for any of them."

It was a hot dry summer, until August, then the rains came. Water, water, everywhere. The water in the old channel was almost up to the railroad track. As the rains stopped and the water went down, the kids made old rafts and played over there.

I didn't know mine were there, but Billy Joe, and Duane, perhaps Merle, were there. They would fall off the raft into that dirty water. The lower that water got, the better they could see the fish in there, and they decided to try to catch them.

The game warden came by and asked the boys their names. Billy Joe told him who he was, and the other boys did the same. They got a lecture and were sent home.

In the afternoon the game warden went back. As there was another crowd of young boys, he asked their names. He came to Duane and asked him if he didn't know it was against the law to catch fish like that.

Duane said no, he didn't know.

The game warden asked him his name and Duane said, "Billy Joe."

He was asked where he lived, and Duane said, "Over there."

The man said, "Show me," so they came to the door.

I wondered what Duane had done.

The man asked me, "Lady, do you have a son named Billy Joe?"

I said I sure did.

He told me he was the game warden and asked, "How come you have two boys named Billy Joe?"

I said I didn't, and he said, "Well, this morning I was over at the old channel, and found a boy fishing who told me his name was Billy Joe and lived here. Now this afternoon I found this one and he says his name is Billy Joe, too."

I asked Duane why he said that and he said that he didn't want to go to jail.

The man told him why they shouldn't be over there and told him to run along, which he gladly did. He told me to try to keep them away from the old channel because that water was so filthy and one of the young girls in our neighborhood had typhoid fever. (She died soon after.)

Chapter 86

August passed and I was very miserable, barely able to do the things I must do. Marjorie, who was old enough now, helped a lot. All the children were in school except Marion.

Again, I hadn't seen a doctor. I had convinced myself that life wasn't worth living and hoped that I wouldn't live through this. Oh, I never said it out loud, and I still pretended that all was well whenever I saw anyone. I am sure all my relatives and old friends knew of my troubles, but I wasn't looking for sympathy, *not me.*

Bill seldom came home in the evenings anymore. I'd sit at the table and play solitaire after the children were in bed. There was another drunken fight, and this time Bill got a month in the jail. That was good news to me.

Someone told Dr. Salley about my plight. He didn't wait to be called. He came and offered his services. He said I wasn't only taking my own life in my hands, but my baby's, too. I promised to call him.

A few nights later I had to get Billy Joe up to go for the doctor. His phone just rang busy. We found out later that his wife had taken the phone off the hook so her baby could sleep. Billy Joe ran all the way to their home, and soon they came back.

Nothing was going right, and I didn't care. Just as the doctor thought the trouble was over, the pains stopped and wouldn't start again. He worked so hard and kept apologizing for hurting me. I kept telling him he wasn't, and it was the truth, I couldn't feel anything.

He said, "I have never lost a baby yet, but I think this will be my first." He kept prying and pulling until he said at last, "It's a girl, but she's not breathing."

He started working with her, and called to the two neighbor ladies who had come to help to get a pan of hot water and one of cold on the table. They did, and he took that baby to the kitchen and put her in one pan, then in the other. At last I heard a little cry and knew my last baby was going to live. I was thankful her life was spared.

Dr. Salley came back and kept saying how sorry he was that he had hurt me so much. He didn't; I was paralyzed from the waist down for hours.

He waited to see how we would be. Of course he knew where the man of the house was, so he was extra anxious about us.

It was the eighteenth of September 1935. While he was still at the house he got a phone call; one of his patients in the country needed him. He told us to be very careful and left pills. He told me they were to take in case I started hemorrhaging, and to be sure to take one every four hours, but not oftener, as they were dangerous to take if one took too many. I sure missed Ma. After he weighed the baby and said she was an even eight pounds, he told me to name her and he would come back to fill out the birth certificate.

All went well that night. The children did what needed to be done. Neighbors had cooked food for them, and I just slept. The next morning my neighbor Ida came first to see that the children were off to school on time. The doctor came and said that all seemed to be under control. He said it looked like I would be all right. Dr. Salley said, "I will be going to a meeting in Salina for two or three days and I'll come by when I get back."

All was quiet. I was just so tired out and sleepy. That evening I started hemorrhaging. Ida gave me one of the capsules and told me to lie real still. I did. The medicine seemed to help. I went back to sleep, and Ida left.

My neighbor Martina came to take her place. Then long before the next capsule was due, I started another hemorrhage. This one wouldn't stop.

Martina was frightened and called Ida back. They tried to keep me from seeing the blood-soaked sheets they were using, but I knew. It didn't seem to matter to me. I must have passed out, because when I woke up they gave me another capsule and I was asleep again.

By morning I had puffed up like a balloon all over, my face, neck, arms, and legs. I was a sight to behold.

They called my sister. She came and yelled, "Call Dr. Cave at once!" He was her doctor at the time.

He came and they told him what had happened. After examining me, he went to the front porch with the ladies. They didn't know my window was open, I guess. Anyway, I heard him say, "She doesn't have a ghost of a chance. I am sure it is uremic poisoning in the worst form." He asked who the doctor had been and why he wasn't here. They told him he was out of town at a meeting, and that it was Dr. Salley.

He went to the phone and called Mrs. Salley and told her to call her husband and make sure that he got back here as fast as he could. He came back and started saying how much trouble that doctor would be in for leaving a patient in my condition.

I told him that it wasn't the doctor's fault, he hadn't even seen me until the week before, and only came out of kindness. I told him it was no one's fault but mine.

He said he would call an ambulance to get me to the hospital.

I said I wouldn't go.

He asked why not.

I said I couldn't pay the hospital bill.

He exploded! "If I was in your condition, there wouldn't be an ambulance around that could go fast enough to suit me," he said.

I insisted there was no use messing up another bed.

At last he left. I was too tired to care what

anyone said or did. The doctor had said I had no chance, so why bother. The hemorrhages still came, but not so severe.

Dr. Salley came back as fast as he could and said, "Listen here, young lady, you are not going to die and leave me to be run out of town, so make up your mind to that!"

He agreed about the uremic poisoning and asked that pitchers of fluids be brought and that I be forced to drink glass after glass of water, juices, tea, coffee, anything to wash that poison away.

Chapter 87

The next day the police chief came again. He had never seen anyone look the way I did. He said, "I'll send Bill home and make him work and leave that bottle alone or I'll break his neck."

I begged him not to send him home, to keep him in jail, but he decided not to.

This time Bill was hateful; nothing pleased him. He did go to work, though. He was afraid not to, I guess.

Someone found a nice lady to come and

spend the daytimes with us. Her name was Pearl Carlson.

I began to improve slightly. The puffiness slowly left, but I had no interest in getting better. I was skin and bones in a month's time and still in bed. I wouldn't try to get up.

Pearl was so good to all of us, and the neighbors could never be repaid. But I didn't want to see anyone.

I did manage to name my baby at last. I called her Aleda Lavone, for my good friend Aleda Moore, who lived in Topeka.

At last the doctor said I was to be carried to a big rocking chair at least twice a day. I tried to talk them into leaving me alone, but they wouldn't. Someone always seemed to be here at the right time to help.

One day an old friend I hadn't seen in a long, long time came to see me. He lived in another state and was here on business. He had talked to some of our old friends and they told him how I was acting, so he came by to see for himself.

I was glad to see him.

He asked, "What's this I hear about you not trying to get well? When did you ever become an authority on whether you live or die? I am ashamed of you. You used to be able to think straight. What's wrong with you?"

He went over to the little crib and picked up my little girl and said, "Lots of people would give anything for a child like that, and you won't try to get out of that bed. Why don't you get up and start fighting for your rights? There's no reason to give up like this. Where is the old gal we used to know?"

I told him she had died a long time ago.

After preaching to me some more, he left, and I haven't seen him since. I know he died in 1956.

Little did he know that it was the fear of another little bundle of joy that was my problem. It wasn't that I didn't love my children once they were here; but I hated their father so much that I just couldn't start over again.

I began to get a picture of myself and what I was becoming. (You will think Granny needed to see a psychiatrist, and you are right, but not the kind you are thinking of.) I needed help badly, but not an earthly kind. I began thinking and talking to the Lord, asking what I should do.

My friend had saved my life; he had made me see myself, and I didn't like the picture. I decided to start making me over.

I think it would have been so much easier if that fear of pregnancy wasn't there. That's what kept me chained in bed all those weeks. (I didn't know that the Lord had taken care of that and there was nothing to fear.)

Anyway, I started trying, and little by little I fought my way back to health again. I was going to change myself or die trying. I took charge of my family again and started doing more, what I wanted to do.

I told Bill that he just had to stop coming home at all hours of the night and causing us to lose so much rest. The children would be so afraid of him, especially Marjorie.

I also decided to go with the neighbors to church, first one, then another. We went in the evenings. Our older children were old enough now to watch the others.

The younger ones were good to mind. I taught them that the Ten Commandments, if obeyed, would be all the law needed. If they didn't steal or cheat anyone and were kind and did unto others as they wanted them to do to them, things would be fine. (That was before they changed the rule to "do to others before they do you.")

I went to my lodge meetings again and started to enjoy life. I was feeling good and found my friends just where I had left them. It had been me who turned away, not them.

Chapter 88

This place needed so much done to it, but there was no money. Bill drank more all the time. The payments on the house had not been kept up, and the bank would soon take it. The porches were in such bad shape, I was afraid someone would fall through the floors. And that's just what happened.

A man who sold extracts, liniments, and the like for the Baker Company, I think, drove up to show me his products. He was a heavy man. When he started to come in the front door the boards broke, and down he went. I thought for sure he had broken his leg. He didn't, but he had a big bruise, and the skin was scraped off. He advised me to get the porch fixed right away and left without coming in. We always called him the Wasatuse man because of a liniment he sold, good for most everything. Billy Joe and I have laughed about that and how scared we were many times.

A friend came to the rescue by telling me to try to get a homeowners loan and who to talk to. I called the man, and in a short time he had men fixing the place. They put on new shingles, new floors on the porches, and refinanced the house. We were to pay it back by the month.

Bill went out of town to work and stayed sober, coming home on the weekends. So life was quiet again.

It seems that while the children were small we were always quarantined for something — measles, mumps, or chicken pox. They got whatever was in style that winter, besides lots of bad colds.

This was the measles year — one after the other took them. I called Dr. Clarkson and told him the kids had the measles. He asked how I knew, and I told him I could smell them, and they had fevers and a fine rash and runny noses.

He said he'd send a sign for the house. The town was full of measles. He called and told the health office to send the sign. A young man came and asked me if any of the children were very sick; he could see them walking around.

I said not yet.

Then he asked if a doctor had seen them.

I told him no, I had talked to the doctor and told him they had measles.

He left and took the sign with him, until he talked to the doctor. Maybe he was short of signs with so many sick. After a while he came back and put it up.

I had already had the measles three times and felt safe. Well, I got them again, and this time they did something to my throat. I have never been able to sing again, and I did enjoy singing so much.

The children were all in school now and always coming home telling me something some of their schoolmates had said to them about their no-good dad and making fun of their clothes. That hurt me as much as it did them. I tried my best to keep them clean. I told them things would get better.

My other friends who were in the same position as we were had the same problems. There was Dorothy P., Clara J., and oh, so many more — mostly wives of war veterans. We clung together now for moral support, and we would pass garments around to whoever they would fit. My sister-in-law Regina did, too. She was a fine seamstress and would make over garments until they looked like new.

Chapter 89

As the children grew older, we needed more room desperately.

After thinking about it, I thought it seemed best to put a basement under the house. So far there was only a hole under the house where the pipes for water were. We had no hot-water heater.

I talked to Dr. Clarkson, told him the plan, and he said fine, just to be sure we had enough ventilation, at least two windows on each side.

Then we asked Grandpa Henry. He said, yes, if the kids and Bill would help, he could make a nice large room down there. So we borrowed some money and got started.

This was the year Dee Dee, or Aleda, was a year old.

They dug that dirt loose and threw the dirt out the only hole they had dug. Grandpa took stones out of the foundation and made windows so they could see. All that dirt had to be shoveled out those windows and piled in the backyard. It was a long, dirty process. The neighbor boys came and helped shovel.

Rock had to be hauled in and a wall laid all around. After that Grandpa Henry built a new chimney from the floor up, in about the center of the house. Then came the cement floor, then a water heater and the new windows. That winter they cleaned it up.

In the spring we got gas to cook with; the boys, their dad, and their friends dug the trench for the gas pipes, saving a lot of money.

We moved the boys down in to the basement room after Joe Burr came and put light switches in. We called it our dormitory. It was a great blessing. We were still crowded but put two beds in one bedroom for the girls. They had been sleeping in the dining room.

For a while all went smoothly. Then one night there was no Bill. He stayed away a week this time.

When he came back I didn't act like he had been gone. I knew trouble was ahead, and from that time on it grew worse. When he was home he was so ill-tempered we wished he would go and never come back.

I began to think of a divorce. I didn't believe in divorce, still don't except in extreme circumstances, but this was extreme.

I told Bill to either shape up or get out,

that I was going to get a divorce.

He informed me that if I did, it would be my last day on earth.

I told him it would be much better than living with him.

And so the battle went on. I wasn't so afraid of him now that the boys were getting older.

Billy Joe graduated from high school and got a job with the city water department. I heard he was starting to drink, too. I refused to believe it. He knew better. Hadn't he seen enough of it?

Duane got work through the summer, and Merle did yardwork. Jean Francis Middleton gave him his first check and some bushes to plant in the yard. He was so proud.

We paid off the loan on the house each month and all the other bills.

In 1939, October 14, Billy Joe got married to a pretty little girl. I liked her very much, but she was one mixed-up kid, with a temper like you sometimes hear about but seldom ever see. Clara was her name.

Bill was furious, and of all things he was afraid they would have a child, and he didn't want to be a grandpa. He was forty-two years old and said he wasn't old enough to be a grandpa.

In September 1940 that's just what did happen. Clara was here with me on September 27 when she began having pains. I called Dr. Bascom, and he said to take her to the hospital and he would be there.

I called Billy Joe and he had to get someone to take his place at work, so we got a taxi and went to St. Mary's Hospital.

When it was time to take Clara to the delivery room, the doctor asked me if I had ever witnessed a birth. I told him I had helped Dr. Colt one time. I had stood at the head of the bed and held the ether pad to the nose of one of my neighbors at her home.

He laughed and said, "Well, come on, Grandma, it's time for a lesson."

So, Kenneth, I was there when you came into the world, and a precious little bundle you were. My first grandchild — I loved you as my own and kept you every chance I got.

Chapter 90

A few weeks later I began to think if I only could find some work, that would be the answer to a lot of problems. That little voice inside said, "The Lord helps those who help themselves." I started looking at the paper closely each night. There was nothing suitable there, so I promised the Lord that if he would help me find work and get me out of this mess, I'd do whatever he wanted me to. I was going to really change.

I wish I could tell you that I changed real fast, but I didn't. That old hate had eaten in like a canker sore and wouldn't let loose. I still despised every drunk I saw and didn't try to hide the fact.

There was a man who went on sprees with Bill, and his poor wife nearly worried her life away, afraid that he would get hurt. She called me many times, asking if Bill was home.

I'd tell her no.

She'd say, "Well, my man isn't, either. I've got the car. Please come with me and try to find them."

Jessie Lee, center, holding her first grandchild, Kenny, with (clockwise from right) oldest son, Billy Joe; middle daughter, Sadie; youngest daughter, Dee Dee; youngest son, Marion; and oldest daughter, Marjorie.

I would say no, I didn't care where they were and that I hoped they would stay away forever.

She would say, "You don't mean that. They may get hurt or end up in jail."

And my reply was, "Okay, I don't care. I won't go barhopping to find any drunk. You go if you want to."

She wanted to know how I could be so hard-hearted. I said it was easy.

A few weeks later it would be the same story with almost the same words. True, I didn't care.

One day my sister was here when the paper came. We opened it and almost at once saw an ad saying, "Help wanted at Ft. Riley. Civil Service examinations will be given at the Headquarters Office."

Sis said, "There is a job for you. Get ready and I'll take you over tomorrow."

I said I didn't think I would pass.

She asked how would I know if I didn't try and find out. She wanted to take the examination, too. She was having the same problem I was: alcohol.

The next day we went, me in fear and trembling.

I came home and told the family what I had done. Bill began telling me that pass the examination or not, I wasn't going to that army post to work.

I said, "Ha, ha, you just watch me and see."

A few days passed and Teresa and I both got letters saying we had passed and would be notified when to come over. We were so glad. She started a week before I did.

Then on March 24, 1941, I was to report at the Quarter Master Laundry, where I had worked through World War I.

PART IV

WORLD WAR II

AND AFTER

(1941-1971)

Chapter 91

The morning of March 24 I was up and ready long before time to start to work. Marion was seven and Aleda, or Dee Dee, was now six years old. They would be in school almost all the time I was away. Marjorie and Faye Marie would be home from school by the time the little ones got here. I knew they would be taken care of, so with new hope I started my new job. I rode over with my sister.

Here I was starting all over again. It was very different from my World War I experience. The passing years had brought many changes. There was no more Interurban — the people rode with whoever would take them and paid by the week or the month for the rides. The work was about the same, and I had the same tired feet from standing on the cement floors. There were many nice people working there. Some people were still there who had been there in 1917. They had stayed on all those years.

I enjoyed the work, but it was hard to come home and do another day's work, the laundry, cleaning, and cooking. I managed somehow with my children's help. They were finding work as fast as they got old enough. We had no lazybones around here.

I felt so sorry for the young men who were in training. Some were so young and had never been away from home before.

All went along smoothly until the bombing of Pearl Harbor; then the busy times came. Bill's brother Donald had been with the navy in Hawaii at the time of the bombing. It was some time before we learned that he was safe. It was a bad time for America.

In 1942 Billy Joe and Clara had another little boy. I wasn't present, Donald Joseph, when you arrived. I was at work, helping fight the Battle of Ft. Riley.

Now I had two grandsons to love. Joe, you were so sweet and had such a nice disposition and were so easy to take care of. I can still see a picture of you in my mind's eye, those bright brown eyes, the timid smile. Of course, I adored both you and your brother, and evenings when your parents went someplace I was happy to keep you.

I remember, Joe, when you were crawling over the floor you would pick up everything you found, and into your mouth it went. One night I was doing some baking and your Aunt Dee Dee was supposed to be watching you.

I thought the floors were safe for you. I forgot I had put some mouse poison on a piece of bacon and pushed it back under a chest of drawers in the corner. How you found that tin lid with the bacon in it is still a mystery. Anyway, you did. You had it in your mouth when I looked down at you.

I was so scared! I called Dee Dee and we put you on the table and I got raw eggs, milk, anything I had ever heard of, and we started pouring it down you to make you sick enough to bring it back up and get rid of the poison.

Then your grandpa came home. He was, as usual, past reasoning with. We tried to explain what had happened, but he thought we were trying to hurt you and kept pushing us away.

Finally, all that we had managed to get down you came up. The smell of it made it certain that you had swallowed some of that poison.

After we got you settled down again I phoned our doctor and he said I had done what was right and you should be okay. Later I found the bacon, and most of it was intact.

I learned a lesson: inquisitive children can

find anything. Dee Dee got scolded for not watching you better.

The young men who didn't want to be drafted started enlisting, and when you were only a few months old your father enlisted and was in the army. He had very little training here in the States and was sent to the South Pacific.

Next your uncle Duane, or Chick, enlisted and was sent to Kentucky. He, too, was shipped out real soon. He was only eighteen years old. How I hated to see him go.

Little did I know what my boys would go through before I was to see them again. Uncle Chick went to North Africa for training and he was in a tank corps. He was one of the men who drove their tanks through the streets of Rome when that city was liberated. It was a proud moment for him.

Billy Joe was in the Philippines in Manila when the Japanese surrendered — a great day for him.

Chapter 92

It wasn't the life of Riley I was living these days. I was up at five A.M. and hurry, hurry, get everyone up and ready for the day. Trying to run a household long distance is not easy. Stormy days were the worst. Sometimes when the highways were icy the cars would go forward ten feet and slide back twelve, or turn off in another direction. I would sit there frozen stiff, so thankful we didn't have a wreck.

Once inside the building we were too busy to worry. I shall always remember those years; they were special to me. All those young men getting ready to go over to a strange country to fight. They were so lonely and scared.

I encouraged them to tell me their troubles. Some were worried about their parents and how they would manage without them, but the ones who were the most miserable were the young men whose wives were expecting babies when they would be so far away. I would tell them that there was nothing to fear, I had eight, all healthy, and that their wives would be okay.

Soon they began calling me "Mom," and telling me their good news as well as the bad. If those babies arrived before they were shipped out, they brought me candy bars, a treat in wartime.

My own boys were good to write to me, but sometimes it was a long time between letters. There was so little they could write. It was good just to know they were safe at that time.

It was hard to buy our groceries, so many items were rationed. We had books of stamps for sugar, meat, and several other items. Each member of the family had a book of stamps that had to last until a certain time. One had to be careful shopping.

Sometimes we had to work double shifts to get the men's things done in time for them to leave. We had very short notice sometimes. We couldn't have time off for anything as long as we could stand up and be counted.

We heard all kinds of rumors — how our prisoners of war were being treated, and when we didn't get letters we wondered if our sons were dead or in one of those awful prisons.

It was decided to take the employees to the theater and show them some pictures of the war. Why, I don't know. It was bad enough without the movies.

Frank, our boss, told me since my sons were over there I need not go if I would rather not. I told him that if the boys could live over there with it, I could surely watch a picture over here. I went, and it wasn't a nice experience.

Of course we had some prisoners of war, too. They were brought to the laundry to work. We were not allowed to speak to them unless it was a question about the work. A lot of them spoke English better than we did, and they were very nice-looking young men.

My job was finding articles of clothing for the men when they got lost in the laundry. It was a full-time job. I enjoyed it and the supply sergeants were very nice to work with. They brought me the laundry tickets with their shortages, and I would try to find the correct item. If I couldn't find it, I got something that would do.

Chapter 93

The war prisoners worked with guards present to watch over them. They looked so lonely, but they were well taken care of over here, not like our boys over there. We were getting the news of how our boys were treated when captured, and it was hard to have kind thoughts toward these prisoners here.

I remember one day when our news had been extra bad, I told a supply sergeant that I thought we were too nice to these fellows, after the way ours were being treated.

He said, "Well, Mom, what would you do with them?"

I said, "I don't know offhand, but I wouldn't treat them nice like you do."

He said, "I just bet you wouldn't."

So next time he came for their shortages, he brought a fine-looking young man and told me his name was Fred and that he would be coming for their things for a while.

I said fine, and I talked with him the same as the others.

We got along fine. After he had come by several times, one evening as the prisoners were being marched out to be returned to their place of confinement, I watched them pass by. What did I see but Fred marching slowly by, and on the sleeve of his overcoat was the word "Himmler." I nearly fell over.

He just looked at me and smiled.

The next time the sergeant came with the tickets, he said, "I am proud of you, Mom, you sure handled Fred well. He thinks you are a very nice lady."

I had sure been fooled and had to admit it.

The sergeant said, "Those fellows are as sick of war as we are, just doing what the bigshots tell them to."

Another day I had received a letter from one of my boys and had it with me. There were a lot of mothers working in this place and when we got letters we shared them, trying to figure out where our boys were. It gave us new hope.

I was so glad that morning to have a little news. When I had a minute I went to show it to some friend close by.

One of those German boys watched us, and when I took my letter and went back to my place, he came by and said, "My mother would be glad to get a letter, too," and I saw tears roll down his face.

Hate him? No, I hated the ones responsible for the war. I felt sorry for the many young people who had their lives turned all topsy-turvy by a few old fools who wanted to rule the world.

Chapter 94

We didn't have bad working conditions. We had a good boss, Frank Walker, who was kind and good-natured. In fact, there was very little trouble and I liked the people I had worked with.

Things at home were getting no better fast. Bill had been drinking more all the time, and it was getting so we seldom got a night's rest. He was getting mean now. He hated himself and tried to make us pay. Many times we were up most of the night trying to quiet him down. He couldn't keep a job anymore and looked like an accident looking for a place to happen.

One day, after one of those nights, I made up my mind to get a divorce.

The children were able to help me a lot. Merle was working at John's Creamery, and

Faye Marie had a job at a café. I didn't like that so much, but her boss told me that he and his wife would bring her home after work, and they did.

I told the family what I was going to do, and they said all right. I don't think they believed me; I had said this before.

I took a day off from work and went to see Judge Kimball and told him I wanted a divorce.

He said, "All right, we have been wondering here how much longer it would be before you woke up."

I asked him what I had to do, and he said nothing. I asked him how much it would cost and he said sixty-five dollars. I told him I would be back with the money.

I went home and counted my little amount of cash and wondered how long it would take me to get that much ready.

But luck was with me. Merle came home and gave me part of his check, and Faye Marie gave me part of hers. So I went back and paid for my freedom.

I hadn't told Bill what I had done; I was afraid to.

It was soon after supper that the sheriff came and told him that he couldn't stay anymore and waited for him to pack up his clothes. He took him to his father's house

Jessie Lee, age 43.

and told him he was under a peace bond and was not to come near us again. The children could go there to see him if they wanted to.

It was wonderful to come home quietly, do my work, and sleep all night without a bad scene. But I dreaded going to the court-house for that divorce. I got two witnesses to go with me, all ready to tell of things they knew to be true.

We went at ten o'clock. We quietly went in and were seated near the front of the room. The presiding judge came in, Judge Kimball talked to him a minute or two, then they asked me to stand up.

I answered two or three questions and the judge said, "I believe I know the facts of this case, so I grant you the divorce, custody of the minor children, and the home, and fifty dollars a month alimony. Good luck to you. Case dismissed." I hadn't needed any witnesses.

Chapter 95

I went home with mixed emotions. I had to manage, so I did. We never know what we can do until we are faced with a problem.

Everyone was so nice about it. I was afraid Bill's folks would be upset with me, but they stood by us. Daddy Henry was a good friend as long as he lived, God bless him. They loved Bill, but knew he was a great problem.

I made up my mind to live my life so that I need not be ashamed to look at myself in the mirror. I would dedicate the rest of my days to trying to guide my family.

I was strict with my girls. I had made up my mind that I'd never let one of them marry a man who carried a bottle. No drunk would make *them* miserable. If I suspected one of their friends might need a prop like that to help him along, I would see that he didn't get my girls.

We were managing fine when Merle turned eighteen and wanted to go into the army like his brothers Billy Joe and Chick. He went to see about it. He got a draft card and was anxious to enlist. I hated for him to go. He told me the man at the draft board said that if I needed him, they would not send him and he begged me not to say that. Merle said he would send me part of his money. When the man called, I told him to let Merle go, I could manage. He went to Colorado for training. He and Dean Niemier went through the war together, the best of friends from childhood.

Now there was just Marion, the girls, and me. Marion and Dee Dee were in school, getting home about the same time I did when I didn't have overtime hours. Those times Faye Marie was home from school, so we managed very well. Marjorie was married to a young soldier from Arkansas. He went overseas, and she stayed with us while he was gone and did most of the housework. She also took good care of the younger two.

We drifted along until April of 1946, then Faye Marie (or Sadie) was married to

Carlus E. Rutledge of Georgia. I hadn't thought that my girls would be leaving Manhattan, and I made a few feeble objections. But C.E., or Tom, as we call him, was a fine young man and God must have sent him our way. He has been a good son to me all through the years.

They had a lovely little military wedding at Ft. Riley with only a few friends. I went with them. They promised me they would live in Manhattan, so all was well at our house.

They stayed with us through 1947. The war was ended, and boys were being discharged fast. I was tired out and not well at all. I could have taken sick leave and found out what was ailing me, but instead I decided to resign my job. I had begun to dread those long rides to work each day.

In September I resigned. After a few days at home I decided to go to Missouri and visit the relatives still living there.

Chapter 96

I went to Holden, where Aunt Cora Belle and Uncle Bert were living, and I stayed two weeks. They took me to Quick City. Some cousins, Ike and Lily York, were living in the house we left when we moved to Kansas.

Such changes! The house was all modernized, and the fishing lake was all gone. The engineers had come with their big machinery and filled it all in, so it was now all dry land.

We drove past the Evans farm where we had been so happy. It looked so strange to me. Of course, it was strange. The years had changed the landscape and also me.

Although I visited Aunt Cora Belle and Uncle Bert several times after that, I have never gone back to Quick City, where I first saw the light of day.

I came home to realize that I better find a job, so I pondered the question of "Where shall I go? What can I do?" Someone suggested that I try the hospital, so I did. The sister in charge of the hiring of people there told me she only had two places at that time, one as a housekeeper, the other in the kitchen. I said I'd like the housekeeping best, so she told me to come to work on Monday morning.

That was the beginning of some of my happiest days. Work straightening the rooms wasn't too hard, and I was so sorry for the people who were sick. It reminded me of the days when Mama had been so ill, with only me to help her. It wasn't long until I was doing things for the patients, which seemed the natural thing to do. But I wasn't supposed to do more than dust, care for the flowers, and be sure the bathrooms were clean.

One day the sister who was in charge sent word for me to come to her office. I went and she said she wanted me to become a nurse's aide. She said they would give me the training I needed.

I told her, "No." I was satisfied with the work I was doing.

She said that I didn't look like I felt well.

I admitted that I didn't.

She told me to make an appointment with my doctor, and that we would discuss the other subject later.

So I went by Dr. Clarkson's office after work, and he told me he was going to rec-

ommend that I see Dr. K. F. Bascom. I
made an appointment and Dr. Bascom told
me that I needed surgery very badly. I
hadn't had proper care after childbirth and
I needed much repair work.

Chapter 97

It was the seventeenth day of February
1947, and the doctor said he would make
all the arrangements and would call and tell
me when he would operate.

I was stunned. I never dreamed I would
have to have surgery.

The doctor got some pictures and showed
me exactly what must be done. After that I
went home and tried not to think about it.

That evening the doctor called me and
said, "I have everything set up for the morning of the nineteenth." He also said I must
come to the hospital the night before. That
left me one day to think about it.

So began my first time in a hospital as a
patient.

My last day at work someone had asked
me which room I liked best on the second
floor. I said, "Oh, I guess 216." When Faye

Marie and her husband, Tom Rutledge, took me to the hospital the next evening I was taken to 216 after I had signed in.

No one could have had better care than I did. I never remembered too much about the surgery. I was asleep when taken upstairs to the operating room, where they finished giving me something to put me in a deep sleep.

Dr. Clarkson gave the anesthetic, and he told me later that just as I passed out, I told them that if they would excuse me, I thought I would take a nap, I was so very sleepy.

Anyway, I had about 4½ hours of surgery. The first two days afterward I don't remember too much about. I was in bed three weeks and enjoyed my stay very much. I also enjoyed all the cards, flowers, and so many visitors.

That doctor was wonderful. He was the last person I saw at night and the first one in the morning. He was so kind and concerned about his patients' comfort. When at last I begged to go home, he asked, "What's the matter, don't you like this place?"

I said sure, but I had to get back to work.

He said, "Oh, you people who are so anxious to get back to work are a doctor's biggest problem." Then he said, "All right, I'll let you go if you promise to just sit around for the next ten days and not try to lift anything. Just walk around a little."

So once again I was home. I was allowed to go back to work in April, but it was just the kitchen this time, just sitting around peeling potatoes, making salads, and drying dishes.

One Saturday the sister came into the kitchen and said, "You can come back to the second floor Monday morning, and I want you to go by town and get some nurses' shoes and two white uniforms." She said that the sister on the second floor would train me for the work. So I became a nurse's aide.

Chapter 98

It did so much for me, helping care for the patients in my small way, and I began to get a new outlook on life. The old hate was slowly seeping away, like the water after a hard rain. It left a compassion and better understanding of life's problems.

I still didn't like your grandpa, it seemed

so hard to forgive him or remember him as he was in the early years. He had sent me some beautiful flowers while I had been in the hospital, and I had refused to allow them to be in my room. Childish? Yes. Foolish? Yes, and just plain mean (I think now). I am sorry about that, but much too late. I also didn't allow any pictures of your grandfather within my sight, and I left the room if he was the topic of conversation.

Sick, wasn't I? I wouldn't have admitted it, even to myself. That's why I couldn't get over my illness. I couldn't see that as long as I didn't completely forgive and try to forget the past indignities, I would never have complete happiness. We cannot hate another human being and be happy with ourselves. I am sure your grandfather suffered much more than I did.

Billy Joe got home from overseas a day or two after Grandpa Henry's funeral. It was a sad homecoming for him. Duane came a few weeks later. I had the home all paid for now except three hundred dollars, and Duane (your uncle Chick) gave me that money. I almost ran to pay it, so I could say that at long last the old place was indeed all mine.

May 1947 — Wayne, that's when you came to us. We all loved you so much, and it is a miracle that you weren't a very spoiled child, with so many of us around to spoil you.

In 1948 your little brother Joe Robert, "Bobby," came along.

You were living on Laramie Street at the time. You were both so white headed and blond. I can still see you in my mind's eye, riding that little tricycle up and down my sidewalk.

The next year we were joined by little brother Ray: three little white-haired boys. So precious, my three little musketeers.

I was still working. Sometimes I had to work the late shift, eleven P.M. to seven A.M. I never liked that; I couldn't sleep daytimes. (Sure can now, though, if I find time.)

Sometime about here Billy Joe was back in the army and his wife divorced us and moved away. Kenny and Joe, that's when you came to live here with me. Your father sent money each month for your support.

It was nice having little boys around again. The only thing was you had too many bosses all trying to tell you what to do or what not to do. It was all for your own good, of course. You were good little boys, though not perfect. I loved you maybe too much for your own good. (It's so easy now to look back and see what I might have done different.) You were so young and missed your parents so much. I became the center of your world.

When my children were young, I had so little time to spend doing things with them. There was so much to do *for* them — work, work, all the time. Oh, I was here in the house and watched over them, settled fights, and put bandages on cut fingers, but there was no time to play games. Just stories at bedtime, and then I was so happy to get them all safely into bed and asleep. Those days passed by so swiftly.

Chapter 99

Then came 1949, a year I could never forget. When I think of those days I wonder how I managed to survive. Where there is a will there is a way, my mother always told us.

One cold January morning I was at work at the hospital; it was nearly two more hours before time to go home. I was tired and thinking how nice it would be to go home and sleep for a few hours. I could go home at seven. About six-thirty I got a telephone call from the Boonville, Arkansas, sanatorium telling me that my daughter Marjorie Lee couldn't survive the day. They told me not to try to get there, as it would be useless. They said they would call me at home.

Marjorie Lee had been there for several months, being treated for tuberculosis. Yes, my weakest child had the same fast kind that took her paternal grandmother and three aunts. She was treated by a doctor in Paragould, where she and her husband lived. That doctor thought she had the flu. She had written me that she had been having the flu, but was better and would be all right.

The next thing I heard, she was taken to Boonville for treatment. I visited her there, and it was a wonderful place. The doctor told me she was responding to treatment and there was no cause for alarm. She had joined the Methodist church there, and those people were so good to her. Her husband had taken a job there at the sanatorium so he could spend a lot of time with her. I stayed three days and came home thinking she would soon be back in her own home again.

Before I left I was told that her doctor wanted to see me. He told me that I must have a test to see that I was free of the disease. They gave me their tests and said it was a sure thing that she didn't get the germ from me. Then I told them of her relatives who had been afflicted with tuberculosis.

So it was a great shock that ninth day of January to get the phone call.

I made arrangements to be away from work, then went home to get ready for the long trip. I called the bus depot and learned that I could leave at noon. About ten A.M. I had another phone call telling me that Marjorie Lee had passed away.

I took Marion with me. We traveled all night. Marjorie's second husband, Homer, took us to his mother's home. Their friends and relatives were very kind to us; I had never met any of them before. But in times of grief, there are no strangers.

We were taken into their hearts and homes, and I shall never forget the kindness of the mortician and his wife and employees. They took care of everything for us, treating us more like family than strangers.

Still, I felt so alone, so far from home and family and friends. It was hard times, those days, for us, and the rest of the family couldn't afford to come with us. I sat there so miserable until, just as the service was ready to start, a delivery man with a huge

arrangement of flowers came and handed it
to one of the men. He gave me the card,
then arranged the flowers on the casket.
The card read "From family and friends."
It seemed to me I could feel their presence
around me, so comforting.

After the funeral, we laid my little girl
away in a beautiful cemetery that is so well
taken care of, in a town of warm, friendly
people.

Marion and I started home, and I felt that
I had indeed left a part of me in Arkansas.

I was soon back home and working in the
hospital, where helping to care for the patients there helped me so very much.

Chapter 100

All went well until May 29. I was working
on the second floor when Sister Rose from
the third floor came to tell me that my
brother had been brought in the night before and was in bad condition. She thought
I should come with her.

The doctor was there trying to find out
what was wrong, what was causing Lynn
such terrible pains. He asked me what I

knew of Lynn's medical history. I didn't remember that he had ever been sick since childhood, so we had no record to go by.

Now while I am speaking of doctors, there are a few things I'd like to say. First, I urge you, my dears, to get your little ones acquainted with your doctor from babyhood, so they won't be afraid when they are older.

Next, there are a few things I'd like you to think about when you go to find a doctor for yourself or family. Remember that a doctor is just a human being, so if you feel that he isn't right for you, that his advice is all wrong, then for your own sake and your doctor's, go find another. Don't just go around saying he is no good just because you don't feel you have been helped.

Every human body is different. What might cure me might kill you. Don't become a pill nut. Your own body will take care of a lot of ailments with rest, right food, and some common sense. All my years I have got along without sleeping pills or the many so-called cure-alls and painkillers.

Take care of yourselves, and then if you need to see a doctor, he will be able to help you. Most of us wait until we are a wreck before having checkups, then find fault because it takes so long to get well again. We didn't get like this in a few days, so why expect our old worn-out bodies to respond to medicine in a week or two?

I haven't always taken my own advice, either. But I sure can't blame that on my doctor, and I have always had the very best ones. Our first one in Manhattan, Dr. Clarkson, took care of all my family, and my mother, grandparents, aunts, uncles, and several cousins, and did a wonderful job.

I have never looked for a doctor myself, for each one I have had has found one for me when he retired. Dr. Clarkson sent me to Dr. Bascom, one of the very best. When he decided to do only surgery, he called me to his office and told me that he would be sending his medical patients to other doctors, and he had chosen Dr. Swartz for me.

He was also one of the best. When he retired, he called me and said that he had sent my records to the Reitz brothers at the clinic and when it was time for my next checkup to call and make an appointment with them.

I did, and have the best of care from them. I look forward to my trips to the clinic; everyone is so friendly.

So you see, I have a special feeling for

doctors. All I have known have been so kind and have brought me through some very bad times.

When I was a nurse's aide, Dr. Jimmy Colt, Dr. Bascom, Drs. Swartz, Nelson, and others, showed me how to do many things for the comfort of the patients and told me many home remedies to use, like gargling with salt water for sore throats, using Epsom salts in very hot water for infected hands and feet.

One of the best nurses this town has ever had taught me so many things about nursing. Miss Dorothy Toy, a wonderful lady, was a good teacher and a friend I am proud to have.

Now back to Lynn. Two doctors worked as hard as they could, but it just wasn't to be. Sister Rose asked if he had been baptized. I wasn't sure, so she asked if I cared if she baptized him. I told her I would be so glad if she would.

He looked at me so pitifully, asking if there wasn't something I could do. . . .

Our sister, Teresa, came, and we stayed with him until evening. He seemed better; we went home.

I got supper for the family, then got a call from the hospital to hurry and come; Lynn was much worse. I called my sister, who said she would be there as soon as she could.

Merle took me at once. I could see that Lynn was much weaker now. Sister came, and we watched him leave us early in the morning of May 30, Memorial Day. It was another bad time.

The doctors asked if they might perform an autopsy to see if they could discover what killed him. Of course, we were anxious to know, too. It turned out to be perforated ulcers.

Our parents had been gone for several years, so it was now Teresa and me, the only survivors. It was a lonely feeling.

We buried him in Sunset Cemetery close to Mama and Daddy and his young wife, who had been killed in a car accident. At least I have been able to take flowers to their graves all these years.

Chapter 101

We had a few more months of peace and quiet. Then in October 1949 another tragedy happened.

My dearly beloved son, Arthur Merle,

was so severely injured that he has had to live in a VA hospital ever since. He suffered a severe head injury and had surgery, at what was called Winter General Hospital at the time.

Some of you are old enough to remember those years, with the long trips almost every night to see if Merle was conscious yet. Tom, Faye Marie, and I kept going, hoping and praying that he would wake up and know us. His doctors told us that they feared he would only be a vegetable, never knowing anything if he did awaken.

The brain surgeon who operated on him was rated among the nine best brain surgeons in the world at that time. He left Topeka before he knew Merle would regain his memory. Those wonderful doctors, nurses, and other personnel cared for him day and night and gave him all kinds of therapy. They saved his life.

His mind is now clear, and he remembers everything before the wreck, except the night it happened. He knows everyone he knew before. He has a speech problem that has been helped a lot, and he lost one hand. He lives most of the time in his wheelchair. He is a good Christian and never complains. He was fifty-three years old on April 27, 1979, and wasn't yet twenty-four years old when he was injured.

Why did it have to happen to a boy who had such dreams of the future and was willing to work so hard? Only God knows that answer.

Chapter 102

Then it was 1950 the year you came, Linda dear, my first granddaughter. You were so tiny and sweet. Each time a grandson was born, Dr. K. F. Bascom would tell me, "Another boy, but the next one will be a girl." Now here at last was my girl. Fifteen grandchildren — twelve boys and three girls. Dr. Bascom delivered nine of you. We all loved that doctor.

Also 1950 was the year Tom's father urged him to move back to Georgia, so you Rutledges began to get ready to go. Oh, how I hated to have you go far away. I thought I would never get to see the children, that's so far away.

It is only natural that children leave to make their own way in the world, and I didn't want to be a bad mother-in-law. I had heard people complain that theirs were always telling them what to do or what not to do, and they resented it so much. I had never had one myself. I didn't want to be a wicked witch, so I have tried not to interfere in my children's lives after they left my home. I made many mistakes, though. I guess that's how we learn to face our problems.

In the fall of that same year, your grandfather Bill became ill and went to the Veterans Hospital, too. He stayed a few weeks, then came back to his sister's home. He was soon back in the hospital.

I didn't know how very sick he was until the hospital phoned me that he would like to see the two younger children if I could bring them there. I took a day off from work, and my nephew took us to see him.

Never before have I seen a person so miserable and sick. His doctor told us he was suffering from cancer and might linger on like that for months.

In the spring of 1951 Faye Marie was getting a little homesick, and wanted us to come visit them. I was anxious to go, but I didn't like to take the children so far away when their father was so sick. His doctor told me to go on, that Bill would be well taken care of and there was nothing I could do anyway.

So we planned our trip to Georgia. My young brother-in-law wanted to go, too, so he would furnish the car. I would buy the gas and food.

We all piled in the car and took off — Dee Dee, Marion, Kenny, Joe, my husband's brother Don, and me. It was a very nice trip; we had fine weather all the way. Little did we know what we were to come home to.

Chapter 103

It had been raining a lot that spring, the lowlands were flooded, and we were lucky to get out of Kansas when we did. We had to go the southern route through Missouri, Arkansas, and on to dry states. One place the roads were closed, and the guard let us through when we told him where we were going.

No one thought of a major flood. Everyone had assured me that if there was a flood, it would never get to my home, so on we went to a fine vacation in Georgia.

We had intended to be away two weeks. Then the radio kept telling us of the terrible floods in Kansas, and how the rain kept coming day after day. Manhattan was badly flooded. We couldn't believe it. One day the phone rang and it was a neighbor girl calling to tell us that our home had come apart and everything was ruined.

Everyone cried but me. I was beyond tears. I thanked God we were safe and not there to add to the confusion. We waited until a friend called and said the roads were open and we could get home. My brother-in-law Don wouldn't wait; he started off by himself to see if he could rescue his belongings.

Tom said Marion could drive his truck home and we could see what was left. Then we could come back to Georgia and find a place to live there. Tom thought I might find work in a local hospital. So we left you, Kenny and Joe, with Faye Marie and Tom. Dee Dee, Marion, and I started that long trip home in the truck. I thought Marion was too young to drive so far, but he did a fine job of it.

We arrived after midnight. The moon was shining brightly on the ruins. We drove up Poyntz Avenue to a hamburger stand across from the high school; they were open, so we got some food.

A young friend of Marion's came in and

asked where we were going, and we told him "home."

He said, "You can't stay there, it's in bad shape." Then he said, "You come home with me. My mom is away, and I'm alone. I'd be glad to have you."

We didn't like to impose, but after driving by home and seeing the door standing open and the furniture piled up along the curb ready to be hauled away, we were glad to accept his kind offer.

(Long afterward I told his mother about it, and she laughed and said, "I didn't know it. He never told me. I'm glad he had you stay." What a wonderful thing to have friends!)

Next day we straightened up our rooms, and after thanking our angel of mercy, we left. I went to my good friend Cleo's home, the best friend one could have. Marion and Dee Dee went to the homes of their good friends until we could get into our home.

I found that Cleo and her husband had gone to our home and gathered up everything washable, taken it to their home, and washed it. Bedding, clothes, everything — thirty-four machine loads they saved for us. First thing I had to do was go to the college and get shots for typhoid and something else, tetanus, I think. They my friends and

I investigated the damage done to my place.

The doors were wide open, wouldn't close. The floors had buckled up and looked as if they would never lie flat again. The only furniture left was a metal table and chairs.

The range was still in place, but had to be inspected. A man from the gas company came and after looking it over said we could use the top burners, but not to try to light the oven. The refrigerator wouldn't work at all.

We were lucky, though: the water had been five feet three inches deep all through the house and the plaster was still in place.

The basement was still full of water. The windows were up. Someone had come into the house before the water got into it, raised the windows, and tried to put the furniture up as high as possible. It didn't do any good, though; it was ruined.

All my family pictures and things we loved were gone forever. The dishes had floated off the pantry shelves and were all over the floor.

The sun had been shining now for days, and the yard was one mass of dried mud. There was not one blade of grass or a weed remaining. It was a desolate sight.

Cleo gave me a washtub, and I bought

soap and disinfectants, a large bucket and mop. I brought some clean things from Cleo's with some pasteboard and wooden boxes, then came home and worked all day for a week.

It was so hard to realize that everything I needed was gone. I didn't even have a clock, just my watch.

I was afraid to stay here without the house being inspected, as the west foundation had given away. I asked the Red Cross if they could send a man to come by and look, just to see if it was safe to be in the house. Well, they have never showed up yet, and I never found anyone, so I stayed here anyway.

Marion and I stayed until your uncle Billy Joe came home from Korea. He got a man named Charlie Cox, who was very good at cement work and laying up walls, and together they fixed the foundation and did a good job. It's still solid today.

I had a little table I liked very much. My great-grandfather Isaac Brown had made it from walnut wood. It had a wooden band around it with carved flowers on it. Its top was as smooth as satin, and the legs had rollers made of white china or porcelain in them. It was a treasure from our home in Missouri. That table was gone, too.

Uncle Chick had loved a piano from the

time he could walk, so Grandpa Henry gave us their piano. It had been his and Grandma Josephine's wedding present. Now it was ruined completely.

An old trunk filled with my treasures was water soaked and ruined. It all just goes to show one that no matter what we may possess today, it may be taken away tomorrow.

Friends that lived in parts of town that hadn't been damaged sent us a few things they didn't need, and little by little we managed to survive.

There were so many kind people. I had been helping Mrs. Umberger take care of her husband before going to Georgia. Now she and her friend Mrs. Kelley came bringing old sheets and rags to clean with and offered to help me.

I told them that their gifts were enough. I could manage now.

Mrs. Kelley said, "Well, I am going to the Red Cross office and have them get one of your sons home to help you."

I thanked them for coming.

In a few days, sure enough, here was Uncle Chick. Mrs. Kelley really had gone to the Red Cross. Most of you know what a worker Chick has always been. He got paint and wallpaper, and soon the old place was safe to live in again.

One day Mrs. Loyal Payne, a lady I had helped care for when she was sick in the hospital, called and said, "My friend, I drove by your home and was so sorry to see your yard in that condition. I am sending a man from our farm in to dig it all up, so you can have grass and flowers again." I thanked her, and soon the man was here, and he really did a fine job. I have had my grass and flowers ever since, thanks to a very kind lady.

Soon came the day when Marion had to go back to Georgia to return Tom's truck and bring back my little boys. I think that must have been quite a trip home. Marion had managed to get an old car and, after it had some work done on it, decided to drive it home. So Kenny, you and Joe, well, you know the story of that trip better than I do.

Chapter 104

In August 1952 we had a phone call from the hospital saying your grandfather was much worse.

I took Marion and Dee Dee to see him one last time. In a few days he was gone.

Your grandfather was brought back to Manhattan and was laid to rest in Sunset Cemetery beside his father.

I attended the funeral with the children. As far as I was concerned, it may as well have been a complete stranger that service was for. I had no feelings beyond wanting him to have as nice a funeral as we could give him.

The VFW post gave the military salute at the cemetery. I heard later that your grandfather had many visits from a priest and had been prepared to leave this world when the time came. Let us all be thankful for that. I know I am. His death was another triumph for Old King Alcohol.

I haven't told you this story to paint your grandfather as a villain. He wasn't. He just didn't have enough backbone or intestinal fortitude to stand up to life's problems.

I have tried to picture for you how a very nice person can become so consumed by the desire for just one more drink that they can become a menace to themselves and everyone they come in contact with. If it had been only my life that was affected, it might not have been so hard. But when we look at the number of people of both sexes who can't get along without liquor, it's terrible. Reports say that about half the people in our country are alcoholics. What can be expected of the little ones growing up today? They watch Daddy and Mama and grandparents mixing their drinks and consuming them right in front of them.

To my girls I say, "If you have a boyfriend who drinks, get rid of him fast. Don't believe that old line, 'I can take it or leave it.' They will never change because they won't admit they need to. If you should marry him, God only knows what troubles you will have. And if you take to drinking booze, your children will suffer. If those hangovers are fun, or make any sense at all, then please excuse me."

Now I am not saying any of you have this horrid habit. I sincerely hope not. If you do, get rid of it before it is too late. It is very easy to get help now. All one has to do is admit it is needed. Then run, don't walk, to the nearest place.

If you have read this far, you will know that I could have done much better than I did. I told you earlier that your grandfather and his drinking buddies ruined my life. Now I know that wasn't true; I did that myself. I took a bushel of self-pity along with a bushel of hate, added a large supply of false pride, and almost destroyed myself. No one can know how blind one can be better than I. I tremble when I think, What if I should have died?

Well, I didn't and I remembered my grandpa Jeff, my mama, and my daddy and the things they taught me. I started to try to change me. It took a long, long time. I had to talk to our Lord a lot and admit I had been so wrong to hate people. I had to ask forgiveness. It wasn't easy to look deep inside and take my share of the blame for the mess I was making of my life. As soon as I felt I was forgiven, it was much easier. The Lord helped me in so many ways.

The main things to guard against as you fight the battle of life are hate, envy, jealousy, and selfishness. Today I am glad to be able to tell you that I have no bad feelings for any person. I can understand their problems, and sympathize, and pray that they realize there is help if they reach out for it. It took me over forty years to learn how to live. That's taking a very big chance, I'd say.

Let's see if we can figure out why this young man of good family, with the same advantages as his other brothers and sisters, became like this.

He was number three in the family, and I imagine that he didn't get all the attention he craved from his mother. I have been told by old friends of the family, and his brother and father, that he was always their problem child. He didn't like school.

He went into the National Guard at a very young age and was sent to the Mexican border when trouble was brewing there.

After he returned, he was one of the first young men to enlist and was soon overseas. After World War I was over, he returned home with great dreams of what he wanted from life. Without much education, he couldn't hope for a high-salary job. When difficulties came along, instead of facing them, he reached for a prop: the bottle.

Maybe if we had never met, he might have done better. Who knows? I realize I had been a spoiled child. I had been taught to work, keep house, but little about life in general. I had been well protected.

I am sure you have a picture of your grandparents by this time. We started off with good intentions, planning as all young couples do. We got lost along the way. I think maybe your grandfather was afraid of responsibility. What do you think?

Chapter 105

On July 9, 1952, Dee Dee, my baby girl, got married. Again luck was with me, and I got another fine son.

I couldn't have finer sons-in-law if I had searched the world over. Dee Dee married Cameron Torgerson, a young soldier who had returned from duty in Korea and was finishing his enlistment at Fort Riley. His home was in Minnesota.

Dee Dee decided she wanted to go to Georgia to be married, so Cameron got a leave of absence from Fort Riley and we all piled into his car and off we went to Georgia, with only a very few days to make the trip. Kenny and Joe, you remember that trip, too, don't you?

Now this part may be wrong, but as I remember, we arrived there on Friday and planned the wedding for Saturday late afternoon. Saturday morning we went to the Winder courthouse to buy the license. We were told "no sale" until the blood test had been taken. The lady who worked there said there was no way they could get married that day, so we left and went to Dr. Russell's office to get the tests.

He said they didn't do that work in his office anymore. Tom told him that the lady had said there was no way to get the tests and buy the license before the office closed at noon. Dr. Russell asked what time the marriage was to take place. Tom told him four o'clock.

The good doctor wrote a note and gave it to Cameron, saying, "Take this note and hurry to the hospital in Athens" — Georgia — "twenty miles away. They will give you the tests and if you hurry, you can make it."

We hurried. We got the tests and back to Winder just ten minutes before the office would close at noon. They were married in the beautiful Baptist church in Winder, Georgia. Tom and Faye Marie were best man and matron of honor.

We started home the next day and arrived without trouble . . . a fast trip with not even a flat tire. Our guardian angels rode with us that time. Soon after Dee Dee and Cameron went to Wisconsin. He was sent to be discharged.

Next my youngest son, Marion, got married, so I gained a son and a daughter. Your aunt Donna has been a dear daughter to me from the very first day. She and Marion lived here with me until they bought their house at 315 Thurston. It has been nice having them live so near. This is the twenty-sixth year she has been with us and has helped us weather the storms of life. We love her and my sons-in-law Tom and Cameron as much as if they had been born into the family.

Chapter 106

The next year, 1953, Dean, you joined us. Your mother and father, Dee Dee and Cameron, came back from Wisconsin so Dr. Bascom could bring you safely into the world. When you were two weeks old, your father got a call to come to Minnesota to work, so off to Two Harbors he went.

Next time I saw you was 1955 on my first trip to Minnesota. Your brother Donald Lynn had arrived. I was so proud of the two of you. It was a wonderful vacation. It was the first time I met your grandma Marie. She is a fine woman, and my good friend.

That year, 1953, was also the year I got

my second granddaughter. December brought you, Diane, a grandchild I could really enjoy since you lived so near me.

Then 1955 brought your sister, Karen. The two of you have brightened my life so much through the years. I remember so many things you said and did. It would have been nice if all my grandchildren had lived so near, so I could spoil them, too.

Diane, you were my little Marjorie Lee come back to me, so it seemed. You had the same loving disposition and looked a lot like she did as a child. You had enough energy for two, always asking, "What can I do to help you, Grandma?"

Do you remember how I put you to work digging dandelions? You and Karen, but she didn't like to work as much as you did, but wanted pennies to buy candy. You took your little buckets and old dull knives and worked away, Diane working fast and filling her bucket two or three times before giving up. And you, Karen, would have a few in your bucket and would always say, "I'm tired now, Grandma. If you pay me now so I can go to the store, I'll come back tomorrow and do some more."

Diane, do you remember the day I had to go see my doctor for a physical examination and you thought it meant I was going to die? After I came home you went out to my flower garden and picked a bouquet of flowers, came in, and said, "Here, Grandma, these are for you."

I asked why, and you started to cry and said, "Well, if you have to die, I want you to have some flowers first."

I thanked you and explained that I was in good health, but loved flowers anytime.

Such precious memories of my grandchildren.

Chapter 107

I had two more grandsons in Georgia now, making five boys there.

David Rutledge, you belong to me. You were my Christmas present; I have the telegram to prove it. It says, "Merry Christmas. Your present this year is a little boy named David Lee." (A child I'm proud to own.) You have grown into a fine man, honest and true. You and your lovely wife, Bobby Jean, know how much I love you, and look forward to the birth of your child in November. You were lucky to find Bobby Jean.

Next came you, Gary, and I was there. I

arrived one day, and you came the next morning. Dr. Russell came and said, "Hello there, Granny from Kansas, where have you been? We have been waiting for you for two weeks." I gave you your first bath. Your mom, Faye Marie, was soon up and all was well. You were number six, and the last. You have done so very well, too, my dear. You and your dear wife, Vicki, have given me my only great-granddaughter, and Brandi Lynn is a beautiful little girl. If I could only shorten the miles between us, so I could see her often. Now don't say, "Get on a plane, Grandma, and come on." You know I won't do that. (Sorry, I am a coward.)

Chapter 108

Wayne, dear, I am still hoping you will find the right girl to marry and live in your beautiful little home with you. If those girls there knew how kind and good you really are, they would be looking for you. The place to find a good wife is a church gathering. Maybe you have a nice girlfriend now; if not, I shall still keep hoping.

Remember the little picture of you that has hung on my bedroom wall so many years? I want you to take it and keep it. It has meant so much to me. I am sure you will always remember the time you were here in the army at Fort Riley. All the good times we had.

I never knew how many boys would come up from my basement on Sunday mornings or any time you could get away from the post; your cousin Kenneth Rutledge, Larry Stone King, and Dale from California and any friends you might bring along. Was a great time, wasn't it? You boys would go by the grocery store and get a sack of food, then with whatever I happened to have, we had some great lunches.

Then came the day you had to leave for "Nam" (as you called it). How I hated to see you go. Your uncle Bill was there to see you off. He said the last glimpse he had of you was when you were trying to help load your company mascot (the donkey) onto the train.

I often look at the pictures you took while you were here. I remember how young and carefree you were — well, "Nam" took care of that. I thank God that He brought you all safely home; so many were killed or crippled for life. No young man should ever have to experience the horrors of war.

I wonder how many people in this country, or in your own hometown, know that it was your scouting party of just a very few men who really discovered the largest tunnel or underground cave, ammunition, guns, food, and supplies found in that war? How you drove the big truck, tank, or whatever, almost on top of it, trying to find your way through land mines, brush, and running the risk of being taken prisoner. When you reported your find, the glory boys took full credit for it. I know how you boys felt after you did all the dirty work for them.

I know those days still bother you, Wayne, but try to forget them. Life has a way of changing things as time passes. I imagine that those who made your life so miserable over there — and I don't mean the enemy soldiers — may not have it so good at home as they did there. They have lost their power over you and are not worth remembering.

I am glad Mike Rutledge came to Ft. Riley for some of his training. He came to visit us when he could. I have felt like he and his brother Kenneth were my grandsons too.

All our family chose the army life, except your great-uncle Donald Foveaux, your cousin Donald Joseph, and your brother

Robert — or Bob. They chose navy; guess they liked the water and seeing the world. I am sorry your brother Ray didn't get to come to Ft. Riley for his training.

You were all good soldiers and I am so proud of you. All my sons and grandsons were sergeants except Marion and Francis. Marion was too young, and Francis couldn't pass the physical examinations. He tried many times. It hurt him so much that his brothers could go and not him. Well, we had our army of sergeants, pretty good for boys right out of high school. Guess the navy doesn't call them sergeants, I have been told. It's about the same rating.

Chapter 109

Now some of my special memories of Georgia are: The long visit with you all. The friends I have there. All the wonderful places your father and mother have taken me — to Atlanta so many times. The zoo with all the beautiful animals, the marble used in the building, the Cyclorama at Grant's Park, and the great Capitol Building with its gold dome. The museum on the top floor showing so many things from long ago. Shopping trips to Atlanta, Athens, and many other towns. The good meals we had. The night we went to the theater to hear Charlie Pride sing. Going to see the old covered bridge built so many years ago. The Okefenokee swamps or just driving around the countryside, seeing the beautiful buildings and homes and the pretty red soil you have there.

The last time I was there, in 1978, they took me to Plains, Georgia, the home of President Jimmy Carter. I hope God will forgive the people of our great country for the disrespect they are showing for him and his family. The comedians with their insults and slurs. Funny? No, it is disgusting to real Americans. If we have no respect for the highest office of our land, how can we expect other countries to, either? Seems to me, we are fast running out of common sense. The more they educate them, the worse they get in many cases. Why blame the presidents for all the mistakes? They didn't make all these problems of today.

It is time to wake up and put the blame where it belongs — on the people who are always looking for an easy way out of things, pushing problems aside until they get out of control, then screaming because they can't be solved overnight. Can you imagine what a sharp pair of scissors it would take to cut all those miles of red tape in Washington, D.C.?

Now, as I see it, Plains, Georgia, was a nice, quiet little town. No banners flying, no big publicity. The people were friendly wherever we went. We drove by the Baptist church where the president and his family go when they are there. We also saw his home. It is very nice — like thousands of homes in Georgia. His brother Billy's gas station was like many others, too. It was just a nice little Georgia town.

I read all the printed stories about Plains, Georgia, and I wonder. Those writers sure saw a different place than I did. I got several picture cards, and Tom brought me some very nice souvenirs to bring home. It was a happy day. Thanks again, Tom.

Chapter 110

Robert Rutledge, my pal, remember that year you came and stayed with me and went to college at K State? The nice talks we had, and how you told me how crazy some of the students were, thinking that sex was the main thing that mattered in life, and how the girls chased the boys?

We can all see where their liberal ideas have come to, not only in college, but in the junior high schools too. The shocking numbers of children who will never know who they really are because their mothers can't truly tell them who their father was.

Whose fault is it? Who knows? My guess is that the older generation is to blame in most cases. They were so busy trying to give their kids everything new that came along, they forgot the most important things, like a paddle to the seat of their pants when they didn't mind, like respect for others and honesty.

I have heard children tell their mothers and fathers that they wouldn't do as told and to shut their mouths, usually with vulgar language and swearing thrown in for good measure. Those parents stand there and take it, acting like they are afraid of the little monsters.

Look now at what we have to live with: yesterday a couple came by my house, saw the little frog that has been on my birdbath for years, and the girl walked over and took it. A neighbor watched her take it and told me about it. It was at noontime, I was away for two hours.

I sit here and wonder how they got that way. The time to teach children is from the time they can crawl. Boys should be taught respect for girls, and girls should be taught modesty and kindness early in life. How times have changed!

I have talked with schoolteachers in several states and they all say the same things. They don't dare correct a child. If they do, they have the child's parents to deal with. Those teachers feel their very lives are not safe in the schools some places, if they try to interfere with the students. Poor blind parents!

I heard a little boy telling of all the mean things he did in school and how if anyone told his mama, she would take his part. He had a habit of finding things that hadn't been lost.

I told him how wrong it was to take things that didn't belong to him and he said, "Well, go tell my mama, she won't believe you." He was about seven years old. That type of child grows up to influence other youngsters whose parents try to teach them right. I wouldn't be a schoolteacher for all the money there is and take the abuse that so many of them have to take these days.

Of course some schoolteachers are not

too good, either. You know what your mother and father would have said if you didn't behave in school? I remember one day when I was visiting at your house and Ray Rutledge came home and said that he had trouble at school. Your dad asked what happened and Ray said, "There was an ugly boy there and he hit me and it hurt."

Your dad asked what you did.

Ray said, "Well, I hit him back real hard."

Then your dad said, "I see. There were two ugly boys in school today."

Ray, who was looking for sympathy, quietly went outdoors to play.

Some parents I have known would have started a neighborhood quarrel over a child's fight. Well, I am preaching again, but I feel so strongly about the little ones coming into the world today.

Will children lie to us? Sure they will, and will continue to unless we can take time to find out the truth and let them know the harm their lie does them and others.

Through all my years I have known so many people and have seen so many things happen. I feel that young people can now see the past few years without their rose-colored glasses and will start to think and try to straighten out their lives and take more active parts in how the country is run.

Anyway, Bob, I am happy that you found your Maggie. You couldn't have given me a more lovable granddaughter. Love you, Maggie, and your son Scott, too.

Chapter 111

Ray and Betty and little Tony Rutledge, no need to remind you how much I love you, because I am sure you already know. I am so proud of your business success, Ray. Hope you get your nice farm like you want it soon. I don't know if I shall get back to Georgia to see it or not. If not, I have all my pleasant memories. You know I love Georgia and Minnesota. But dear old Kansas is home sweet home to me.

Now my Linda, my girl, I am so sorry we haven't had more time together. I treasure the hours we have had, and thank you for all the lovely things you have done to make my life more pleasant. I hope you and your husband, Tom, will have many happy years of life together. When the going is rough, just pray about it and things will straighten out.

I love Tom, too. I am happy you get to

go so many places. It's nice to travel, and I do enjoy the cards you always send me. It is like sharing your sight-seeing with you, honey. Be very careful flying that airplane. I hope you get to come to Kansas.

I guess Casey will be back from Italy soon, and I hope Mary Dale and Patty find whatever they are searching for in life. You know we can make our lives happy and sad; it's up to each individual. If we have health, a good mind, and are willing to work, we can make ourselves happy.

May good luck be with your California girl, Denny, and her family. Wish I could get to know her, too.

Chapter 112

Now back to Minnesota and you, my Danny boy.

Wish we had time for some nice long talks. I am proud of your ambition and your carpenter skills. When you finish your apprenticeship you will have rewarding work. You have had more accidents than any boy I know, but so far you have come through in fine shape.

You say you think life is like a big puzzle. How right you are, my dear. Life is like a puzzle, and the pieces fall into place each day, and the giant puzzle lasts all along life's way. No use to worry about tomorrow, let us live for today, for today will soon be tomorrow and tomorrow will be yesterday. The past will be gone then forever; we can't change one little thing. We must look to the future with faith and whatever changes it brings. We can try to do better each day.

God will, if we ask him, give us the strength for whatever may come, so let's put guilt and confusion behind us. Once we ask and are forgiven, we can start the new day with joy and accept the fact that we are all sinners saved by God's grace. Then we can have a cheerful smile to light up our face to greet anyone we may meet anytime or anyplace.

You will make a good life for yourself, Danny, you have all the ingredients. I am so glad you and I can communicate. We have had our great talks ever since you were a little boy. Keep playing that guitar and singing; music is good medicine for us all.

Chapter 113

Now Don, let me tell you how I remember you as a little boy. You were a beautiful little baby, and so good-natured.

I visited you in Silver Bay when you were about a year old, and you would sit on a rocking horse you and Dean had, and you rocked yourself to sleep time after time. I was so afraid you would fall off and be hurt before we got you safely off it and into bed. You never did, though.

You were a well-behaved child all through the years, and your love of music was apparent at an early age. I have enjoyed listening to both you and Danny play, and David, too. I am sure he will have great success with his drums.

I have all the letters you have written me, Don, the ones from school and while you were overseas in the army. I have some pictures you drew me, too.

Six of my grandsons have risked their lives for our country. I hope the other six won't have to go to fight such a useless, senseless war as the one in Vietnam.

I am proud you went and came back safely. I think it was much better than deserting not only our country, but relatives, too, like many young men did. I imagine they have suffered much from their rash decisions. Right or wrong, we are Americans first, last, and always. You have done well, Don, since you returned, with your job, your music, and now you have your own little home. Now find a nice little wife and what more can a fine young man want?

Chapter 114

David Torgerson, you have a bright future ahead of you. You have done so well in school and with your music. Don't give up playing your guitar. I know you love your drums best. It's hard to realize you are nearly grown up; the years have passed so quickly.

It was so nice all the times you all came here to visit. You know, I doubt if all of you get to come again at the same time, or your Georgia cousins, either.

I remember when your parents were married in Georgia. As we were leaving to come back to Kansas, Cameron said, "Now you folks bring the little Rebels and come visit us real soon."

Tom replied, "Yes, it won't be long until we are bringing our little Rebels to play with your little Yankees," and how true that was. Kansas was the meeting place.

You know how much I love that old Lake Superior. It never looks the same any two days. It's like a moody person, one day bright and beautiful, the next day dark and gloomy and unpredictable. The lake always reminded me of my old home in Washington. How I treasure all those nice vacations I have had in Minnesota with you and the ones spent in Georgia. I was a lucky lady.

Remember 1970 when we took the long trip in the camper your dad built? Thirteen wonderful weeks of vacation, going through so many states. We visited in Dover, Delaware, along the way, with Kenneth and Joanie and boys, and then on to Georgia. The beautiful weekend in Florida was the first time I got to pick oranges off the trees. We spent the day and night in Orlando, Florida, with Gordon and Marion Fears, spending a day in wonderful Cypress Gardens. Then we went back to Georgia. After a few days there, we started home, coming back through Texas, and stopped in Oklahoma to visit your aunt Janet and uncle Ray and their sons. Then we came on home to Kansas. It was such a beautiful trip. David, you may remember all except Florida. You stayed in Georgia while we went there.

Another highlight of my life was the night we went to Duluth to see *The Lawrence Welk Show*. They were on tour. I enjoyed it so much. All days were special in Minnesota. The trips to visit your uncle Ray and aunt Marion at their home in First Sawbill Landing and later in Ely, Minnesota. I enjoyed the trips to Tofte to visit your grandparents there, and the times we went to the very old town of Two Harbors.

That's where your parents lived the first time I came to visit; it seemed like another world to me. The houses were built too close together, like people huddling together to keep warm. After seeing the snowdrifts there, I think that must be the reason for putting the buildings so close together. Cold, cold weather.

Now my dear David, you have the brains, the personality, and good looks, so use them in an honest way. To thine own self be true, and you will have many advantages in life. Use them wisely.

Dean, Don, Danny, and David, we have

shared so many good times together. Don't forget them.

Dean and Becky, I'm so glad I got to come to Silver Bay for your lovely wedding. Now with two sons of your own, you have a big job ahead of you.

Chapter 115

Darrel, let's see what memories I can share with you. After your father came home from Korea, in his last years of army life he started working with some plumbers. He had some experience in the army, I think. He lived here with me until he married your mother; then they moved into their home. I was visiting Minnesota at the time. Your father got a job, civil service, at Ft. Riley, and they bought the home where he still lives. I was working when you were born. You were a fine healthy little boy. I didn't see much of you. It was too far for me to walk, and I didn't have much time after work. Your folks were busy, too, and the years slipped by so fast.

I am sure you remember the family gatherings we have always had, the big dinners, and how your mother always made the fruit salad we all liked so much. We had such nice picnics at Uncle Chick's when Aunt Dee Dee and Uncle Cam and the boys came. Those vacation times were great. Nearly always around the Fourth of July we would go to Wamego for the evening, after our picnic.

I always felt that you, my dear, had been shortchanged from the beginning of life, with no brothers or sisters to play or fight with and a mother who was sick so much of the time. Oh yes, you did have two half-brothers, but they were nearly grown up when you came along and so not much of a comfort to you. Wish I could have been with you more. I might have been able to help you over some of the rough places.

Anyway, you are doing fine now at age nineteen, working steady, and I am proud of you. I like your girlfriend Susie, too. I think she understands you better perhaps than anyone. I hope you will always feel free to come to me any time I can be of any help to you. You know I love you, even if I don't see you often.

Chapter 116

Billy Joe's son, Donald Joe, I miss seeing you. I know you are busy and it's a long way up here. Remember the fun we used to have? You know you are always welcome. We used to be very close. I know we have disagreed on some things, but that's all right; maybe I was wrong sometimes. You were my little boy for many years, remember?

Marion's daughter, Diane, you and your husband, Greg, have been so good to me, and I sure thank you for all the nice things you have given me.

Your son, my great-grandson Robert, is a most precious gift. It was a fine compliment that he chose my birthday for his wedding day, and our celebrations each year are a joy to me. I don't need presents, just love.

Marion's younger girl, Karen, you and your husband, Joe, had such a beautiful wedding. You have done well, too, building your own home, doing all the work yourselves and both working all the time. Isn't easy, I know.

Karen, dear, I am proud of your bowling scores, and I watch for the evening paper the night the scores are printed. You, your mother Donna, and Diane are all very good. Of course, your mother has the best record so far. Something to work for, hmm? You girls were good softball players, too.

My, but you grew up fast. It seemed one year you were my little girls, then the next teenagers, then young ladies and married. Time has passed so swiftly, but you, Karen and Diane, will always be my little girls, just growing older and dearer to me. I am proud to have your husbands for my grandsons.

Counting them and Tom Clavin, I now have fifteen grandsons. All my granddaughters are married, so this is my final count, I hope. I plan on you all staying married; you know the service says "for better or for worse." I listened to Billy Graham last night and he said there is no such thing as a perfect marriage. They all take a lot of patience and TLC. Karen and Joe, I am looking forward to the arrival of your baby. Boy or girl, it will be beautiful.

Chapter 117

Now to my great-grandchildren. I want to tell you that I am well pleased with all twenty-three of you. As I am with my great-great-grandchildren — all five, with number six on the way.

I hope you will all finish high school and decide on what you wish to do with your lives and then prepare yourselves for it. The world has no place for lazy people. If you have a job to do, do it well or not at all. Have pride in your work.

Education will be needed more in your lives than ever before, so learn all you can. Learn to read books early in life. It is not only a source of knowledge, but a source of pleasure, too.

Avoid strong drinks and drugs like you would the plague. Don't listen to those who tell you how much fun they are. They only scramble your brains, and you run the risk of retarded or deformed children. It isn't much fun for the taxpayers who have to pay out millions of dollars trying to correct the miseries of these poor children because their

Jessie Lee at 84 with her great-granddaughter Julie Marissa Rutledge, 21 months. Behind them is a tatted bedspread by Jessie Lee on display at the Riley County Historical Museum.

parents mistakenly thought they were having a good time.

Just do the best you can, trust the Lord, and you will have good lives.

My mother used to sing a little song to us. It went like this:

Do not look for wrong or evil,
You will find it if you do.
As you measure to your neighbors,
So they will measure back to you.

How true! Be kind and nice to others and they will do the same for you.

Chapter 118

It is strange how grandmothers remember the little things their grandchildren did or said as small children. Little do they suspect the things that stay in the mind of Grandma. One day you will know. When you are old and alone these memories will mean so much to you. All the pictures kept from babyhood on, how precious they become.

I am not sorry that I don't have a lot of money to leave you. That makes too many problems. I have watched so many things happen over money while staying with sick people through their last days. I have seen strange things. People who had the least worldly goods seemed to be the ones most loved by their family and friends. It was a pleasure watching all the kindness shown to the patient. The others, who would be leaving a lot of money and possessions behind, were barely tolerated. I have had several old ladies tell me that they knew their families were so anxious for them to hurry up and die so they could start fighting over what they were leaving. It seems that if you want love, it is safer not to have too much money and to live only as long as you can manage to care for yourself.

I don't have to worry about the money part, just the helpless part. When the day comes that I can no longer look after myself, then I am ready to travel to the Promised Land. Hope you will all meet me there someday.

If any of you have any questions you want me to try to answer, ask me. If I happen to have any little knickknacks you would like when I am through with them, tell me — I will put your name on it. My Bible with the red leather cover is for Diane; she asked me long ago. The antique rocking chair I love is for Marion's wife, Donna, if she wants it. Otherwise you may tell me now, or forever hold your peace.

Billy Joe's son Kenneth and his wife, Joanie, I am glad you chose to come back to Kansas to make your home. It is so good seeing you often, and Kenny, I need you. What would I do when all my little gadgets need fixing or the roof starts to leak? And Joanie, you always come along just when I need company. God bless you.

Your son, Kenneth Jr., I have enjoyed having you stay with me these two weeks. It gives us time to become really acquainted.

Thanks so much for the yardwork you did for me. I would have been until next Christmas getting it all done. Always feel free to come by for a visit.

Your brother, Tony (Anthony Duane) Foveaux, we must spend more time together. Seems you have been a busy boy now that school is out. Get on that old bicycle and pedal it this way. Who knows, I might have a candy bar hidden someplace. I am praying that something can be done about your hearing problem. I am sure one day it will happen. Do you remember when I couldn't hear? It kept getting worse and worse; it was a bad time for me. I sure appreciate what the doctor did for me, and the day will come along when they will be able to fix your ears, too. Believe it strong enough and it will happen.

Faye Marie's grandson little Tony (Charles Anthony) Rutledge, I remember how you watched over me when I was sick and at your grandparent's home. You were always asking, "Do you want something, Great-Granny?" I bet you still have that tatted snowman I made for you. Keep it, honey, there will never be another just like it, because that one was made with some thread and a lot of love for you. I am still waiting for you to come to Kansas to find me. Remember when I left to come home to Kansas? You said, "I am going to come to Kansas and find you." I'll try to wait around here until you are old enough to do it.

Chapter 119

I am thankful for each year, each month and day I am permitted to be up and busy. I look back on a life of hard work, and I have decided it was good for me. I'm just thankful that I was able to get it done.

I have done many things that weren't necessary, like all those scrapbooks. I know they will be put into the trashcan, but I had so much fun fixing them. I keep thinking of all the books I am going to read and my records I am going to play. They are trash to many, but treasures to me.

It wasn't easy to raise eight children, and I made many mistakes. I can see them so plainly now. I am proud of my children. They *are* and always have been a great blessing to me. They are always looking for ways to make life easier and more comfortable for me.

You may ask, "Grandma, did your kids always do what you wanted them to?" The answer is *no*, they didn't. Then you might ask, "Have they hurt your feelings sometimes and disappointed you?" and that answer is *yes*. I am sure most mothers can say that they have been hurt many times by their children. Not that they mean to hurt you; it is mostly thoughtlessness on their part, I think. Anyway, my wounds heal quickly and I forget them very fast.

So I count my blessings:

1. I am glad I am a Christian (a poor one, perhaps). I try to do the best I can as I see it or understand.
2. I am thankful for each member of my family and the many friends who have known my faults and failures and have stood by me anyway. I can truthfully say I would rather have a million friends than a million dollars.
3. I am thankful for my health, and that we have good doctors who help us stay well.
4. Too many other things to mention here.

Chapter 120

When I was young, I used to wonder why old people wanted to live on. I wondered what they thought about, how they filled their days. What did they do for entertainment? It seemed to me it would be a very dull existence for them.

Well, now I know. Here I am an old lady. I can't say I feel much different than I did ten years ago. I don't move so fast and it takes a little longer to do my work. So what? I don't need to hurry anymore. I didn't realize how gradually old age came along.

I think it starts when younger people begin to ask, "How old are you, anyway?" That's one thing I seldom do. Aunt Cora Belle would have told me, "Now that's a rude thing to do, Jessie Lee. It is none of your business." You see, she was one of the ones who never said how old she was until she was ninety. Age is a touchy subject with some ladies. Why, I can't imagine. If you live, you must get older, and you can only camouflage it so much, so why bother or worry about it?

Now that I have become one of the many so-called senior citizens, the elderly, old folks, or whatever, it all adds up to the same thing. Is it bad? No, I don't think so. I keep plenty busy. I enjoy so many things, living in my little house by the side of the road, trying to be a friend to all. Now is the time I have looked forward to for so long.

I used to tell the ladies I worked with that when I retired I would get me a rocking chair, a canary bird, a lot of books. Well, I got the rocking chair and couldn't find time to do much rocking. The books piled up — more things to dust. I got the bird, he was wonderful, sang most of the time. I named him "Bing," after Crosby. Well, he died, and I got another, called this one "Jimmy Dean," then one day he went to bird heaven, too. So I gave up and concentrated on my flowers, and they have stayed with me. Now my pets are all plastic, ceramic, or pictures — much cheaper these inflation days. So you see, it gets easier all the time.

I keep myself well entertained. I do my housework, or give it a lick and a promise, anyway. I work outside all I can with the garden and flowers through the spring and summer. I visit friends and neighbors, attend Bible classes and church, go to lodge meetings and the two clubs I belong to. I

Jessie Lee tatting with great-granddaughters Christy Kitterman (left) and Wendy Waddell.

take nice trips each year. I write many letters to friends in other states. My family knows how I enjoy sending and receiving Christmas cards and messages; they send me stamps so I can continue this pleasure. I play my records, which I have a good variety of. I listen to the soap operas of my choice on TV. I know many people disapprove of those, but I think there are many good lessons to be learned from them. They picture life like it really is in these United States, sad but true. They show up human frailties, and if one uses good sense, they can profit by watching all the mistakes those people make. If they remember, it is only a story, like reading a book. Anyway, after watching all their problems, mine are too small to be mentioned.

I still tat or crochet doilies for friends and family. I don't crochet much anymore. I can make three tatted doilies with the thread it takes to make one crocheted. Any of you girls wanting a tatting shuttle? I have several, and if I should leave some tatting half-finished, which one of you will finish it? Linda? Rebekah? Only two of you have learned the stitch. I'm always glad to try to teach anyone wishing to learn.

Next I love to read good detective stories. I like to see if I can find the real crooks before the end and figure out how they got so mean. If that isn't enough, I play a few games of solitaire. Because I'm lonely? No, because I like to.

Do I get bored and lonely? Very seldom. I think everyone has days when they feel a little down, but if they look around them and see their blessings, they will soon be looking up again. I like to just sit and re-member old friends and good times of the past. So many have left this world now.

I realize that my happy days can come to an end anytime, so I shall just enjoy each day. It is wonderful to be a citizen of the USA, and Kansas is the best place on earth.

I would like to live long enough to see the moral standards of this world change for the better, to see people stop voting for someone because he belongs to a certain party. All my life I have been a Democrat, as you all know. They have some rotten apples among them, too. Some of them will do anything to win, so try to vote for a good, honest person. I believe there are many around who could do wonders if they were allowed. Jimmy Carter is the best president we have had for many years, or would be if he had some help, and I think our Lord will help him.

The young people I have become acquainted with seem to be thinking in the right directions. I feel that homes will become better places for the new babies who come into the world. They will be taught right from wrong. There are many, many wonderful young people who will be the leaders of our country soon. I pray they will do a better job than this generation has. If not, we are all doomed. Many of our politicians these days depend on bottled spirits to lead them. They must enjoy themselves, and the rest of the world be damned. And it has been, in many ways.

Now that I have perhaps bored some of you to tears, it is time to retire from my attempt at writing and give you all a rest. No more preaching, no more advice. I leave you all on your own. You all have good health, your fair share of brains; now get busy and make a good life for yourselves. I know you won't all agree with my ideas; so be it — I didn't expect you to see all things through my eyes. If you find anything written here that you believe or like, remember it; if not, forget it. It's as simple as that. So far, you all seem to have done real well.

Bye now,
Grandma

P.S. Many thanks to Mr. Charles Kempthorne, who encouraged me to attempt this review of some of my years. Often when I was ready to quit, I remembered when a job is once begun, never leave it until it is done. Now I have finished, and he deserves a lot of credit for his patience, reading this and giving me advice. Thank you, Charlie.

And many thanks go to Maureen Conn, the sweet young lady who typed all this for me. I know how hard you worked. God bless you, Maureen.

Jessie Lee Brown Foveaux

Epilogue

After I finished this book about my life, I thought I should never attempt another one. I went about my usual routine — going to Church, Rebeka Lodge — VFW auxiliary, the American Legion Auxiliary, and the like. As I never did try to drive anything other than a wheelbarrow, I was taken to these meetings by my friends, who came for me.

Today I am feeling very blessed that at ninety-eight years of age I am able to attend to my own work almost as well as at age seventy or eighty. Of course, I am slower, but I can manage my own personal business affairs, write my own checks, and do light housework. I have had help from Home and Hospice or Home Care, Inc., one or two hours twice a week for the past two years, but only because I had a broken hip and other injuries. I have stayed here in my own home by myself, cooking for myself, and it is wonderful to be able to visit with my friends and family. I am very glad that my granddaughter Linda Clavin came to be with me for an extended visit. She is a very good companion.

Since my life in Manhattan began in 1910, I have come to love it here. It will always be my home. My mother, father, and brother are buried here in Sunset Cemetery, along with many other relatives. My sister Teresa and her second husband, Mr. John Palonis, moved from Manhattan several years ago to Cherokee Village, Arkansas, a very beautiful place for retired people to live. She still lives there today. She isn't able to come here and I can't go there. I have not seen her in years. Seems my traveling days are over.

I used to go to visit my children in their homes and stay with them for several weeks. Then I would awaken early one morning with a great longing for my own humble home in Manhattan, Kansas. So at breakfast, as we were gathered around the table, I would announce that I was heading home.

I came there by Greyhound bus, so all I had to do was pack my belongings and come home. I loved to travel by bus. Over the years, I met so many nice, friendly people traveling that way. Some of us wrote letters for years, then no more. Perhaps their number was called and they have left this world for a better one.

I would like to live long enough to see our world become more like it used to be. Remember how many of our best boys and girls have had very short lives because they went to fight in wars to defend our way of life. Now look how we are repaying them. Please wake up, America. Once we were the most respected nation on earth. Have you noticed how the country has deteriorated since World War II? It's as if we have no respect for anyone or anything and no morals. We must remember that God made us all. Black, red, white, or yellow — we are all of us as good as the other, as long as we try to live good lives.

Next year, I will have been watching this old world turn for one hundred years. I still read the papers and watch news on TV. I think our country will become great as soon as people stop, look, and listen. Children need lots of love and care to grow up as good citizens. Before we can clean up our country we must clean up ourselves. Look this over, my children. At my great age I won't try to tell you what to think, but please don't throw away your common sense. That comes with you when you enter this world. Keep it and use it. It comes in handy sometimes.

I have been blessed my whole life long

with loving parents, beautiful children, wonderful grandchildren and great-grandchildren, and many faithful friends. This is the last of the story. God has greatly blessed me and my family.

Jessie Lee Brown Foveaux
April 1997

www.falmouthpubliclibrary.org

FALMOUTH PUBLIC LIBRARY
www.falmouthpubliclibrary.org

FALMOUTH PUBLIC LIBRARY
www.falmouthpubliclibrary.org

FALMOUTH PUBLIC LIBRARY
www.falmouthpubliclibrary.org

FALMOUTH PUBLIC LIBRARY

**PLEASE DO NOT REMOVE
DATE DUE CARD FROM POCKET**

By returning material on date due, you will help
us save the cost of postage for overdue notices.
We hope you enjoy the library. Come again and
bring your friends!

FALMOUTH PUBLIC LIBRARY
Falmouth, Mass. 02540-2895
508-457-2555